Caroline Darian is [illegible] t. This pen name is v[illegible] ly a contraction of the [illegible] s, David and Florian. [illegible] o say in every interview: 'Without them, I'd never have been so strong and determined to be able to undertake everything I've done to hope that chemical submission would eventually be recognised as a real public health issue in France. This cause is very close to the hearts of all the three of us: David, Florian and myself.' Caroline is a senior communications manager in a large company in France. She is also the daughter of Gisèle Pelicot and Dominique Pelicot, whose trial in Avignon for the chemical submission, rape and trafficking of his wife has made headlines all over the world.

Caroline's response to the devastation her family experienced was to help others by raising awareness of this frequently undetected public health issue: domestic chemical submission. She founded the charity M'endors Pas (Stop Chemical Submission: Don't Put Me Under) to campaign for better overall support for victims and systematic training for all professionals concerned.

Praise for

I'll Never Call Him Dad Again

'A riveting read. A shocking story. A mighty woman.'

Oprah Winfrey

'Astonishing … A woman who is hell bent on surviving and tackling her mission.'

Emma Barnett, *The Times*

'It is a story of resilience, lucidity and courage, told with force'.

Agnès Poirier, the *Guardian*

'An antidote to doubt, shame and silence.'

Anna Leszkiewicz, the *New Statesman*

'Everyone should read it … Makes you want to reimagine how we defeat rape and sexual assault.'

Jenna Price, *Sydney Morning Herald*

'Absolutely compelling.'

Brendan O'Connor, *RTÉ*

'Caroline Darian's powerful, compelling prose turns the pain of her struggle into a call to action that will leave every single reader changed.'

Afua Hirsch

'[Darian] has given up her peace and anonymity, to fight for the voiceless, and to educate the masses. To wake us up.'

Jameela Jamil

I'll Never Call Him Dad Again

CAROLINE DARIAN

Turning Our Family Trauma of Chemical Submission into a Collective Fight

LEAP

First published in the UK in 2025 by LEAP
Updated edition published in 2025 by LEAP
An imprint of Bonnier Books UK
5th Floor, HYLO, 105 Bunhill Row,
London, EC1Y 8LZ

A CIP catalogue record for this book is available from the British Library.

Paperback ISBN: 9781785126031
Hardback ISBN: 9781785125973
Trade Paperback ISBN: 9781785125980

Also available as an ebook and an audiobook

3 5 7 9 10 8 6 4 2

Design and Typeset by Envy Design Ltd
Printed and bound in Great Britain by Clays Ltd, Elcograf S.p.A.

MIX
Paper | Supporting responsible forestry
FSC® C018072

The authorised representative in the EEA is
Bonnier Books UK (Ireland) Limited.
Registered office address: Floor 3, Block 3, Miesian Plaza,
Dublin 2, D02 Y754, Ireland
compliance@bonnierbooks.ie

www.bonnierbooks.co.uk

Shame must change sides.

For my son, nephews and nieces.

‘Once something has been written down
there’s no escaping it.’

LIONEL DUROY *VERTIGES* (2013)

Preface: After the Trial

January 2025

I thought I was ready for the trial.

I was ready to face Dominique Pelicot again, the man I'd last seen on Friday 10th July 2020 – a sunny summer's day – at our family home in Mazan. I was ready to look at him, to listen to him, to show him my hate, my pain, my boundless distress.

I used to consider myself his daughter. Not any more.

I would never call him Dad again. I had no idea who he really was – this man who had raised me in a dark morass of horror and lies.

I was ready, along with my brothers and my sister-in-law, Céline, to act as civil parties to the prosecution, alongside our mother, Gisèle. We would stand together, pooling our strength, confident in our two lawyers, facing it all: the court, the ranks of the accused, their 49 defence lawyers – and this man, now a stranger to me.

I was ready for the violence of what we would hear and see: for the brutal mechanics of the justice system; for the theatrics of a trial that would make history; for the virulent attacks and the shameless justifications; for the contemptuous questions and the insolence of those who would attempt to redefine rape out of existence; for the farcical saga, with a cast who would appear to take delight in feigning sincerity and inventing excuses for their cowardice. I had steeled myself to attend a hypocrites' ball.

I'd had four years to prepare myself for this trial, after investigators spent 30 months meticulously chronicling the nature and extent of the crimes of Dominique and his accomplices, who had raped my mother more than 200 times. Four years to digest the fact that over 20 men would be absent from the court, their lives going on as normal, because it hadn't been possible to identify or track them down.

I knew every detail of the 380-page charge sheet. I was familiar with the rhythm at which the accused rapists had been pulled in, ten at a time, throughout an entire year, and the stomach-turning contents of the resulting interrogations. I'd shaken my head over each and every one of the conflicting accounts offered up by Dominique concerning Gisèle and, on a number of occasions, myself. I'd absorbed a mountain of psychological and psychiatric reports.

I'd seen the vast majority of the stills taken from the appalling videos showing my mother being raped and violated. I knew by heart the sickening, systematic and precise procedure followed by the perpetrators of these crimes. I carried a map in my mind of all the places where they had taken place, including in my own home.

I'd studied the two photos where I could be seen, lying on my left side, curled up on myself, like my mother in all the videos, unconscious, a quilt pulled back to reveal my buttocks dressed in beige underwear that wasn't mine, and yet was visible on both images, taken in different places at different times. The photographs came from Dominique's hard drive and had been dated as sometime between 2016 and 2019. I'd seen the photoshopped images where I was labelled 'My slut's daughter'. I was aware of the file folder called 'My naked daughter', which he had tried to delete and wipe clean.

I wanted answers. I wanted the truth to come out in its entirety, for my mother and myself. I'd braced myself to demand the truth owed me, come what may. Whatever the cost, I would pay it, even at the price of my mental health.

But I wasn't ready. Not by a long shot.

I wasn't ready for the trial, for the way it played out: the torrent of falsehoods spouted by this man and his 50 co-accused; the breakneck speed at which the proceedings ran; the sensation of standing alone, feeling totally vulnerable, racked with pain and plagued by unanswered questions; and, finally, for being faced with a parent incapable of admitting what he had done to me and unable to explain what had motivated him.

I'd spent four years condemned to sleepless nights, wrestling with doubt, anger, bitterness and incomprehension. At the same time, I had found a sense of purpose in campaigning to bring the problem of chemical submission out of the shadows.

The four months of the trial brought the darkest depths of the human soul to the surface, stripping bare all pretence to humanity. Day after day, my father lied, offering up spurious justifications and partial confessions while refusing to admit the whole truth. He insisted he had been a good father and husband, a good father-in-law to my sisters-in-law, Aurore and Céline, and my husband, Pierre, and a good grandfather to his grandchildren.

My mother, brothers and I had agreed that the trial should be public. It would be a fitting end to Gisèle's four-year-long trek along a hard road with her children's support. We knew that if the full extent of his cruel and savage deeds and the dark underbelly of chemical submission were revealed, then things might change. Whatever the three years of campaigning had achieved, the trial would accomplish even more, reassuring victims that they could come forward and speak the truth, no longer be alone and no longer deliberately ignored. Our message – that we refused to stand by and let rape and sexual violence flourish – would finally be received loud and clear.

Had I expected the trial to capture the rapt attention of the entire country and the rest of the world? Had I anticipated the crowd pouring into the Avignon courthouse every day to follow the proceedings and sing my mother's praises? Had I foreseen the upsurge of support from women's associations across France, the countless articles by feminists, sociologists, psychologists, writers, politicians and journalists? Had I thought that the Mazan rapes would precipitate a moment of truth for the patriarchy, for rape culture, for the conspiracy of silence over the absence of any true notion of consent in French law? Not in the slightest. Nobody did.

I've been told how brave and strong we were. Truth be told, we simply refused to be crushed underfoot. We were ready to pay whatever price was necessary to raise the flag of resistance and give a rallying cry for the courage and strength of so many others.

I've been told we won. What, exactly, is unclear. The lasting consequences of all we went through remain to be seen.

I've been told our voices were heard, our grievances understood, and that the law, if not the entire justice system, will change as a result. I'm still waiting.

I've been told that the truth was revealed, that no one believed Dominique Pelicot and his fellow accused, that the arguments offered in their defence failed miserably, that the shameless attempts made to defend and rationalise their acts – mistaken rape, unwitting rape, accidental rape, merely technical rape – were met only with contempt. But can it really be said that the collateral victims of the trial gained access to the whole truth? What conclusions have been drawn from the trial in terms of what happened, what always happens and what must happen in the future?

Over the course of the first few weeks of the trial, I grew accustomed to watching Dominique sitting smugly in the dock, perched above the entire courtroom as if he were the one presiding over the panel of judges. I grew tired of listening to him shamelessly spin tales, his story shifting time and again, especially when it concerned me: no, it wasn't a photo of me but of my mother, Gisèle; yes, it was me, but he wasn't the one who had taken it; and so on, and so on. Each day plumbed new depths. Each day leeched a little more life from me.

There is much that needs to be remembered about the four months of this trial, especially when thinking of those yet to come: the men who were never tracked down, and who may never be judged for their crimes; the insistence with which Dominique and the rest of the accused proclaimed their astonishment at being pursued; the way they downplayed the gravity of their deeds; the pleasure so many took in turning up to ridicule us; the arrogance of those accused who had been released on bail and were free to insult and intimidate us outside the courthouse; the revelation of the victims from *before*, whom Dominique may have sexually abused and against whom he may have perpetrated even more serious crimes from 1990 to 2010, before Mazan became his focus.

When I thought of the judicial stumbling blocks we had encountered, the many injustices encountered, the risk that all might be forgotten, the abundant evidence that this trial was simply a first step – in the words of the prosecution, 'the foundation stone of an appalling memorial that is far from complete' – I knew I had to take up the pen once more and update my book.

This is the story I have to tell.

It's the story of a rapist – in fact, a serial rapist – who not only weaponised drugs via chemical submission but made it his very signature in crime after crime throughout most of his life.

It's the story of a system whose failings allowed Dominique to avoid a judicial reckoning for decades, free to do what he liked, flying under the radars we blithely believed could spot his kind.

It's the story of a family built upon lies, of treason against the fundamental laws of humanity, of a clutch of children ground underfoot, left abandoned by all, including the justice system.

It's the story of my life in the shadow of a now notorious sexual predator: of being his daughter; being manipulated; being deceived; being drugged without my knowledge so that he could abuse me; being denied recognition as his victim; being told to content myself with his absurd assertions of innocence; being denied any form of consolation; being forced to fight on alone in the face of universal indifference; and being determined to surmount this tragedy, win back the right to a normal life and avoid being perpetually paralysed by trauma.

I've now spent four years living in a black hole. What will the years to come bring? How can I escape this whirlwind and find firm ground upon which to stand? The trial ended on 19th December, but the verdict was never going to bring me closure, especially given how disappointing it proved. True, a page of history has been turned, but our family's tragic tale, having played out in such a public forum, will leave us scarred for life.

More than anything, this is the story of four years in the wilderness, fighting to make visible how widespread, how common, chemical submission has become. It's been an uphill battle. I've had to learn how to explain a complex, poorly understood phenomenon to unbelieving or unwilling audiences. I've searched for weapons to fight back against what is almost a perfect crime. I've thought long and hard about how to ensure that my awareness-raising organisation Don't Put Me Under can have a real impact. I've struggled to remain optimistic when discovering the sheer magnitude of the number of victims – the known, the not yet known, and those whose suffering may never be known.

* * *

On Monday, 18th November 2024, my brother David told the court that every member of our family remembered where they were and what they were doing on the 2nd November 2020. That was the day my mother called Pierre, my husband, and then each of her three children in turn to explain what she had just learned of Dominique's arrest and the charges against him.

No one in the family escaped being crushed by this avalanche of horror and deceit. We all had to claw our way out and find a new way to define ourselves.

We all feared losing our minds, our health, our marriages, our family ties, our ability to work, our confidence in raising our children, our ability to have a normal social life.

Who was this man who we thought we knew so well, who we trusted so blindly? What had allowed him to treat us this way? What were we to do with our memories? How could we relate to the past we had shared with him?

How had he come to arm himself with drugs that we all assumed – like everyone else at the time – were only encountered in nightclubs, crowded bars and drunken festivals? How could the entire family have failed to notice anything over the course of a whole decade – and even longer than that, now we know that his criminal activities had begun long *before*?

Which of us had the slightest idea at the time what chemical submission truly entailed?

Writing kept me afloat. I wrote for myself as a form of therapy. I have yet to stop. I came to prize the silence and solitude that came with crafting my thoughts and emotions into phrases.

My pages became the first edition of *I'll Never Call Him Dad Again*, which was initially published in France in April 2022, after months of isolation and investigation, as well as writing and revising, all with the support of my publisher. For weeks before it was released, I was anxious about how it would be received by the public. I was taking a step into the unknown and I could not predict the repercussions it might have for me.

In the weeks after it hit the shelves, dozens of heart-rending cries for help reached me through social media. That's when I realised that my instinctive response, that sharing my account of what had happened could help others, had not been a mistake.

The book was an important first step, but I couldn't stop there. Telling my family's story was not an end in itself. It had to serve a purpose – one I found in creating Don't Put Me Under the following year.

The founding members of the organisation were all convinced of the urgent need to raise awareness of chemical submission. By the time the trial started, we had persuaded many that it was far from uncommon and a key factor encouraging and facilitating rape, sexual assault and domestic violence. We hammered home our stark message: rather than being an isolated case, the Mazan affair was a symptom of an alarmingly widespread process of abuse and control.

Introduction: Before the Trial
August 2024

A trial that will go down in the history of the French judicial system is about to open in a courthouse in Avignon. The nature and scope of the case are both unprecedented.

Starting on the 2nd September 2024, it will run for four months. The criminal court of the Vaucluse department in Southern France will remain in full session five days a week. Fifty-one men, one of whom is my father, stand accused of crimes of the aggravated rape of my mother over a ten year period. Each and every assault took place without my mother's knowledge, due to her having been secretly drugged by my father – a horrific and seldom talked about type of abuse called 'chemical submission'.

My father is also charged with having solicited men through an online hook-up forum to have sex with his unconscious wife, whom he had rendered oblivious by administering her a cocktail of prescription drugs. He asked for no money in return. His only condition was that he could film it all.

Eighteen of the accused are currently in custody while thirty-three are out on bail and will remain so until the final verdict is rendered on the 20th December 2024. During the four months of the trial, they will be able to pop in and out of the courthouse, then return to the comfort of their homes in the evening, just like any other model citizen. I will have to tolerate being seated near to them, week after week, with only a few chairs separating us.

If found guilty, the accused face up to 20 years in jail. Forty-nine lawyers will defend them, pleading variously against charges of aggravated rape, rape in association with others, attempted rape with several aggravating factors, sexual assault in association with others, invasion of privacy by taking and distributing images of an individual, invasion of privacy by taking and distributing images of an individual of a sexual nature, and, finally, possession of pornographic images of a minor. The list of charges alone demonstrates the unimaginable nature of the crimes committed.

In France, those who have suffered from an alleged crime can become civil parties to the prosecution, allowing them to participate actively in the trial alongside the state prosecutor, who represents the public interest. There will be five civil parties in this trial: my mother, my two brothers, my sister-in-law and me.

Twenty thousand pictures and videos taken by my father illustrate the full extent of the chemical submission inflicted upon my mother. The courtroom will have to wade through this cache of horrors, built up over many years as my mother was abused dozens and dozens of times. There are even photos of me, taken without my knowledge, the full implications of which remain to be determined.

It will be a public trial, not a closed court. Given the numbers expected, the courthouse has been specially configured to provide a room for the accused, a second for the lawyers and the civil parties, and a third where the press and the public will be able to follow a live feed of the proceedings. For months, my mother, my brothers and I have been quietly preparing ourselves for this ordeal.

In September 2024, we will be called to the witness box and be cross-examined by a horde of lawyers and the members of the court. (In France, this type of crime is judged by a jury composed exclusively of professional magistrates, who can all intervene.) Our lives will be scrutinised and dissected in detail – lives that we would have nonchalantly described as banal only a few years ago.

We have no illusions about what awaits us: we will be

plunged back into the nightmare of my father's deeds and laid bare before the public gaze.

There will be a brief respite after the opening of the trial, because my father, Dominique, will not take the stand until mid-September. In the weeks that follow, the rest of the accused will be questioned. After that, the lawyers for the prosecution, the civil parties and the defence will have the floor.

We know that reliving the tale of my mother's persecution will be painful, but beyond that we don't know what to expect. None of us has lived through anything like this that might give us a clue as to how to prepare ourselves. What has befallen our family can only be termed cataclysmic. My father not only drugged and raped his wife for almost ten years without her knowledge, but he also served her up – for his sheer voyeuristic pleasure, with no money changing hands – to more than 80 random strangers, most of whom he recruited via the hookup site Coco.gg. The site has now been closed down by the authorities; having been implicated in several criminal cases and the subject of over 23,000 complaints, it was finally taken down on the 25th June 2024.

I bear a crushing double burden: I am the child of both the victim and her tormentor.

For four years now, I've been trying to find a new way to exist. In a single instant, all the certainties that had underpinned my life were taken from me, leaving me on the edge of a vertiginous gulf. What kind of a future can you build when your past has been so comprehensively demolished? When even your present – the mundane routine of daily tasks – has become unrecognisable? For the two years following my father's arrest, my family found itself stumbling through a maze where each door we opened revealed not only new horrors, but also a timeline of crimes that stretched ever further into the past. Each discovery brought more unanswered questions.

I have tried, without success, to unearth and understand the true identity of the man who raised me. To this day, I reproach myself with having neither seen nor suspected anything. I will never forgive him for what he did for so many years. Nonetheless, I'm still haunted by the image of the father I thought I knew. It lingers on, deeply rooted inside me.

I've had no contact with him since the 2nd November 2020. But as the trial date approaches, he appears in my dreams during the few hours of sleep each night grudgingly affords me. He talks to me, we share a laugh, we are together. Then I awake, and the nightmare of my new life reclaims me.

Yet I miss my father. Not the man who will appear in the dock, but the one who looked after me for 42 years. Way back in the *before* – when his monstruous nature was still unknown – I loved him so much.

How can I remain calm at the thought of confronting him in court? How can I reconcile the anger and shame I feel with the stubborn empathy that comes with being someone's child? I'm told he has been moved from prison to prison three times over the past four years: from Le Pontet (in Avignon) to Les Baumettes (in Marseille) and then to Draguignan. He is now kept in solitary confinement. Conflicting voices arise in my head. One whispers to me: How is he coping with his new environment? Does he suffer from our absence, from the isolation, from the violence of the prison world? The other is harsh, dismissive: What else does he deserve, given all he has done to Mum, to the family, to each and every one of us? Leave the deviant to his own devices. Let him reap what he has sown.

My father is a criminal and I have to live with this stark reality. I have to accept being torn between the love I once felt for him and my need for truth and justice.

Sometimes I am filled and crushed by a feeling of abandonment. Why are you so far away, Dad? I thought I had finished mourning my father. In reality, a little girl still exists within me, one who hasn't yet let go of the paternal ideal.

I fear that I'll never be able to hate him. Perhaps the trial will finally put a definitive end to my period of mourning. For while he's still alive, I may never be able to tell him, face to face, that he has ruined an huge portion of my life, extinguished the spark I had *before*, crushed underfoot the natural confidence I once had in men.

What we have endured has at least served to highlight a phenomenon largely underestimated in France: chemical submission is far more widespread in the familial and social sphere than anyone thought. It is the preferred weapon of sexual predators, and yet no reliable statistics exist concerning its use. In 2020, the year my father was arrested, nobody was talking about it.

Chemical submission is present at all levels of society and is deployed against a wide range of victims: women, sometimes men, and even children, babies and the elderly. Poorly understood, barely visible in official statistics, it is rarely diagnosed and is neglected by the professionals and support systems supposed to help victims of abuse. Everyone has heard of GHB (gamma-hydroxybutyrate), the 'date-rape' drug, but who is aware of the risk of being chemically subjugated by a spouse, lover, relative or friend companion with the contents of the family medicine cabinet?

Recent scandals, covering a gamut of crimes from femicide

to incest, have shown that sexual violence is generally underpinned by a power dynamic that transforms an isolated act into a systematic practice. Chemical submission is no exception to this rule: the majority of victims are female, and in over 70% of known cases, the doping is a prelude to sexual assault. Above all, this type of violence typically happens within the confines of the home.

A study undertaken by the French National Agency for the Security of Pharmaceutical Products, based on a sample of 727 complaints filed with the police in 2021, revealed 82 cases of chemical submission. The victim was generally a woman between 20 and 30 years old (69.5% of the cases concerned women, but it is likely that the true percentage is much higher). The number of traumatised victims to come forward in such cases willing to endure the gruelling judicial system must be rare indeed. The substance used by the perpetrators was most often – in 56% of cases – a prescription or over-the-counter medicine: antihistamines, anti-anxiety medication, sleeping pills and opioid pain-killers. Sleeping, allergy and cough medicines are prized by abusers for their sedative and muscle-relaxing properties. The next most common substance, used in 21.9% of cases, was MDMA, otherwise known as ecstasy, whereas GHB was only noted in 4.8% of cases. The aggressor was often someone well known to the victim (41.5% of cases) and the assault often took place in a domestic setting (42.6% of cases).

It is important to note that the victims themselves are often unaware of the abuse; just as in my mother's case, they have no idea what is being done to them. Speaking out and seeking help in situations of domestic tensions or violence is difficult, but when the victim can barely remember the assault or the identity of the aggressor, it becomes almost impossible. Chemical submission flies below the radar, affording abusers a sense of impunity and encouraging them to continue. Months, if not years, can go by before anyone notices anything.

Generally speaking, the sexual predator seeks to paralyse his victim, switching her off like he would a lightbulb. She becomes a doll, a plaything in his hands. For some experts, the popularity of chemical submission is partly linked to abusers sidestepping potentially guilty feelings by telling themselves their victim felt nothing and won't be troubled by memories of the assault after the fact.

But the victim doesn't forget: her body and her unconscious mind bear the scars. Nor can she escape the secondary effects of the substances she unknowingly ingests. Still, calling out the abuse is almost impossible. Reporting a rape is, in and of itself, incredibly difficult. Add to that no conscious awareness of the assault and no recollection of what led up to it, then all that remains is doubt and silence.

The victim – her very status as such uncertain in her own mind – is faced with a sense of confusion and powerlessness. Inexplicable health problems assail her with perplexing regularity. But a doctor, having not been trained to recognise the symptoms, will never consider the possibility of chemical submission, assuming he or she has even heard of it. Even hearing reports of abnormal fatigue, memory loss, unsteadiness and frequent nausea, a doctor won't think to ask about an excessive consumption of pharmaceuticals... And even if the question were asked, the victim, kept in a state of ignorance, would answer in the negative!

On the rare occasions when chemical submission might be suspected, GPs lack the diagnostic tools. A toxicology test is the only way to determine the presence of doping agents, but they are not a standard practice in primary care. The initiative is left to the victim, doomed to seek out proof at her own expense. All alone, faced with the time-consuming, complex and costly process of gaining access to testing facilities and experts, the most likely outcome is that the victim, exhausted, simply gives up and a formal complaint never makes it to the police.

There is no isolated, standalone solution to this problem. To provide help to the victims, we must equip those in primary care with the means to spot the abuse. For the crime to be reported, let alone justice be done, we must encourage and facilitate exchanges between the medical, police and judicial systems.

No real progress will be possible until chemical submission is treated not simply as a police matter but a public health issue. And a widespread one at that. Studies show that chemical submission causes falls, comas, memory lapses, insomnia, unexplained weight loss, addiction, unwanted pregnancies, traffic accidents and post-traumatic stress disorders – the health of society is at stake. Health authorities, social work agencies, the police, the judicial system, civil associations: without their coordinated intervention, the problem will persist. There is a collective responsibility, and it must be recognised.

In September 2022, a few months after my account of my mother's case was first published, I decided to join forces with others committed to this fight. A year later, we launched a movement called 'Stop Chemical Submission (#Mendorspas): Don't Put Me Under' to create awareness of the problem and help prevent it. My objective now is to go beyond the case of my mother and give a voice to all the invisible victims.

In taking this initiative, I have had the great good fortune to receive the support of people whom I admire greatly. One such person is Leila Chaouachi, a pharmacist and expert in pharmaceutical monitoring from the Centre for Evaluation and Information on Pharmacodependence in Paris. Leila is in charge of the annual study produced by the National Agency for the Security of Pharmaceutical Products. She spearheads the effort to spread best practice nationwide in the medical treatment of victims of chemical submission. She played a key role in revealing to me the extent to which my mother's case was not an isolated one.

I reached out to a host of media personalities to ask them to spread the news of this initiative across social media. I would never have been able to do so without the help of a number of individuals who lent me their support from the very outset. Without my friend Arielle and her entire team, I would never have obtained the media exposure and gained the momentum that allowed me to launch #Mendorspas ('Stop Chemical Submission: Don't Put Me Under)'. Together, we were able to craft a campaign to raise awareness of the impact of chemical submission in the domestic sphere. We called for a well-resourced training programme for healthcare professionals and the creation of an interministerial working party tasked with improving victim care and support, particularly at a primary care level.

The Joël Guerriau affair hit the news on the 14th November 2023. A member of the Senate, he was accused of attempting to drug Sandrine Josso, an elected deputy for the Loire-Atlantique region. Under the pretence of a party to celebrate his re-election to the Senate, Joël is said to have invited Sandrine to his apartment. Astonished to find herself the only guest, Sandrine claims that Joël secretly spiked her glass of champagne. Dizzy and nauseated, thinking that she might be having a heart attack, Sandrine managed to flee the apartment.

Picked up by a taxi driver who found her condition worrying, Sandrine called the emergency services and had herself taken directly to a hospital. When examined, she exhibited the typical symptoms of someone who had consumed drugs: dilated pupils, a dry mouth, a general wooziness. A toxicology test revealed traces of MDMA in her blood. Joël Guerriau was subsequently charged with 'administering a substance without the victim's consent capable of altering her judgement or depriving her of free will in order to commit rape or another act of sexual assault'. If convicted, he faces up to five years in prison.

The case has yet to come to trial. If the charge is proved, it will illustrate an alarming fact: chemical submission can be inflicted by a colleague from the office. The person trying to dope you could well be a friend. For the first time, the subject of chemical submission had been raised within the world of politics, and by a woman with the courage to speak out, loud and strong.

I immediately reached out to Sandrine to invite her to become a figurehead and spokeswoman for our association. My reasoning was simple: success will come from transforming individual trauma into collective action. We instantly joined forces. Our objective is to encourage victims to come forward, telling them they will be listened to, believed and provided with support. It's critical to reach out to those who don't have the advantage of being a known public figure with access to the media.

Sandrine was tasked by the prime minister with leading a government enquiry into this problem. The recent dissolution of the National Assembly on the 9th June 2024 stopped the enquiry in its tracks. We don't know if it will continue under the next government.

The final words of this preface must be dedicated to the strongest, most admirable woman I know. My mum. She's currently 72 years old. From an early age, she had to face tough times and moments of despair. She lost her own mother when she was barely nine years old. She died in January 1962, in the heart of the winter, 'as a result of a long illness', in the parlance of the time. Today, we would be more direct: she had widespread cancer. Such a loss leaves a lasting scar on a child's life and to a certain extent moulds her future. My mother drew from it her iron will, her determination to face up to whatever challenges she encountered. Her love for life is unconditional, no matter what it throws her way.

After the revelation of my father's crimes, my mother left the home they had shared without a moment's hesitation. She emptied cupboards, took down photos, discarded furniture and packed up boxes almost without shedding a tear. Despite the shadow cast over the 50 years she had spent by her husband's side, she retained her dignity throughout. Fragile and exhausted, yes, but quietly stoic too.

She had no choice. She knew she had to go, even if it meant leaving her friends, her neighbourhood, her village, the countryside and mountains she adored, to face living alone in an as yet unknown destination. The two of us are very different. I'm an open book, my emotions there for all to see. She is like a mediaeval queen – chin up, head high, never the slightest complaint. Towering over the ruins, she is the real heroine of this story.

Over the last two years, Mum has become the dominant figure of our family group. Yet she was the principal victim of my father: drugged, abused, thrown to the wolves. Tirelessly, she has talked it all through with her children, hearing us out as we process it for ourselves. On the mornings when anger or despair refused to let me out of bed, Mum was always there to encourage me to get up, get out, to interact with others, to keep life going.

She followed her own advice. She moved to a new region where she knew no one, learned to live on her own, took up driving again, oversaw the upkeep of her house and took charge of all the paperwork – all the things that were once my father's domain. She has made new friends, developed an entire social network, resumed exercising and cultural outings, all while remaining discreet about her life *before*. She is joyful, funny and full of energy. Her goal is to regain the right to a normal life, to get on with things in a place where she can avoid the over curious. Not once did she lose heart, not even the day when she was told that one of her rapists was HIV-positive. Her innate elegance extends even to refusing to say a bad word about our father.

These last few months, Mum has insisted that I need to take more care of myself. I threw myself body and soul into the fight against chemical submission in France. To stand up in public and in the media's glare is no picnic. Advocating for a cause so long ignored requires a high tolerance for failure and frustration.

I find strength in my mother's personal credo: 'Never lose faith in life and in the wonders it has in store for you.' It may sound naive to some, but it has kept me going.

Mum was the one who decided that the trial should not be held in a closed court. Thanks to her, the public will be able to hear and see everything. She wanted the 50 men facing charges to be exposed to the public gaze. A closed court would have been a comfort to them. They should answer for their crimes in front of the largest possible audience. We talked long and hard about this before she made her decision. I respect her choice, for all my anxiety about having our family's history exposed by the media. Details will be seized upon and lies will be spread. I have no idea how to steel myself for such scrutiny. Who would not feel anxious at losing control of the intimate details of their life?

In her own words, my mother has thrown off her shackles, with a little help from my forays into the public sphere. She says it's impossible to help other victims if you're ashamed of being one yourself. As she said to me: 'Caroline, you have my thanks for all you have done on behalf of the victims of domestic chemical submission. In this fight you have chosen, I will aspire to be your worthiest champion.'

In the midst of destruction, my mother's hand remains firmly in mine.

To discover the extent of this destruction, read on.

Sunday, 1st November 2020

Tomorrow my son, Tom – all of six and a half years old – has to wear a mask to school. So we rehearse putting one on. Once, twice, ten times.

I post a photo of my masked boy on Facebook. Seconds later, my father pitches in: 'Poor little Tom. Going back to school will be a little weird this time around. Best of luck from your Grandad, who loves you more than anything.'

My last ever exchange with my father. I just don't know it yet.

At that point in time, life was so simple. At 42 I had a job I loved, a husband, a child and a house. All normal things I took for granted, like the feel of solid ground under my feet. That each day flowed smoothly into the next didn't strike me as a privilege that could be snatched away. The future was full of hope, not danger. My husband, my son, my career, my hobbies, my parents, my brothers and my friends were the threads that spun together to form my life. An ordinary life. You could even have called it banal.

Only those who have had it torn from them know how precious the banal can be.

Monday, 2nd November 2020

I drop off Tom at school, just in time. I give him a kiss and rush back home, make myself a coffee and log into work. One meeting, then another, then another. The faces change, but there's no escaping the screen.

At 11am, my husband comes home. Pierre works when the rest of us sleep. He sends a text to my father: 'I've just seen the route for next year's Tour de France. How about this as a new family goal: you and your grandson, on the slopes of Mont Ventoux on the 7th July, cheering them on? Up for it?' He makes himself a snack and goes off for a snooze.

When he wakes up, he's missed two calls, both from landlines in the south of France. Two voicemails are waiting for him.

This is the tipping point. The moment when everything

changed, like when a hospital calls because your name is down as the next-of-kin. As often as not, a life-shattering moment has a voice, a face. You never forget the bearer of bad tidings. Pain engraves their appearance and the way they spoke deep into your memory. You always remember, down to the slightest detail, where you were and what you were just doing *before*.

For me, it came as a ricochet. My husband took the bullet first. A message from my mother: 'It's me. It's urgent. It's about Dominique. Call me. Please call me.'

Dominique my father, weighs nearly 16 stone and has difficulty breathing. Since COVID is still raging around us, Pierre immediately assumes he's in the intensive care unit, struggling to draw oxygen through a tube. But that doesn't sit with the other message, which is from a police lieutenant in Carpentras, a town not far from my parents' home.

Pierre calls my mother back.

'What's the matter?'

'Dominique is going to prison. He was caught in a supermarket trying to film up women's skirts. Not once but three times. The police held him in custody for 48 hours. While they had him, they confiscated his phone, a bunch of SIM cards, his video camera and his PC. What they found… it's serious. Really serious.'

My mother called Pierre. Not me. She couldn't bring

herself to tell any of her children. But she knew she could count on Pierre. She knew he could take it, no matter how bad the news.

They talk it through. Pierre convinces her to call her three children, starting with me, knowing he would be by my side.

Still not quite able to believe what's going on, Pierre calls the number the police lieutenant had left. And our whole world comes tumbling down.

'We've found videos showing your mother-in-law asleep, clearly drugged, with men abusing her. Sexually.'

He can't believe it. The words open a gulf, an abyss. They drag Pierre into another world, one of sordid crimes and lurid media coverage. A world that was foreign to us – unthinkable, even, in the context of the lives we led *before*.

The lieutenant goes on, calmly delivering the facts in his possession. They pile up, an alien presence, a crushing weight we will have to carry for the rest of our lives.

The abuse of my mother has been going on for at least seven years. The first images the enquiry has dug out from my father's digital hoard date from September 2013. The number of men who have abused my mother is impossible to believe:

'The current count is 73. Right now, we've managed to identify 50 or so. The youngest is 22, the oldest 71. They range across all classes and professions – students, pensioners, even a journalist. Your father-in-law organised the whole thing, taking photos and filming everything that took place. I have to tell you, the images are hard to stomach, even for us. And there's still a lot we haven't gone through yet.'

The police have been working the case day and night for six weeks. They feared for my mother's life, being drugged so often and so deeply, given she's just short of 68. The lieutenant signs off with: 'You've got to look after her. She's going to need as much help as you can give.'

Pierre focuses on a single goal: take what he has been told out of the house. He is determined to give me a few more hours before I, too, am wrenched into this awful new world. With all my attention focused on my computer screen, I don't even notice him as he crosses the room and goes outside.

In his car, Pierre calls his sister Véronique, Tom's godmother. He asks if she can come round to help that very evening. They agree on a plan that will keep me in the dark for as long as possible.

It's nearly 7pm when I finally escape the demands of my job and realise that my husband has brought my son back from school. I suggest getting a Japanese takeaway. Just as I'm heading out, the doorbell rings. It's Véronique, who sidles in with her usual good-humoured smile.

'I was in the neighbourhood.'

Tom rushes to her and she wraps him up in her arms.

I set off to the Japanese restaurant. As I'm driving I call my mother, but she brushes me off. I get the nagging feeling something is not quite right.

Back with the takeaway, I place the bags of food triumphantly on the dining table. I hear my son laughing with his godmother. Nothing out of the ordinary, provided you don't know that the ordinary is running out of time.

In the kitchen, Pierre has a solemn, serious look. He asks me to sit down.

My mobile phone rings. I see it's my mother, and assume she has finally found the time to talk to me. Behind Pierre, the clock on the cooker is visible. It's 8:25pm.

Later on, I learn that those who experience sudden trauma can often only recall a single, isolated detail – a smell, a noise, or a particular sensation; something infinitely small, which expands to take up all the available space.

For me, it's the clock on the cooker. Twenty-five minutes past eight, etched in stark white. These figures symbolise the threshold I'm about to cross. My name is Caroline Darian, and in a matter of seconds my banal, contented, normal life will come to an end.

I can still hear the hesitation in my mother's voice. She asks me if I'm safely home and if Pierre is there with me. She insists that I have to be sitting down in a quiet spot before she can tell me what she has to say.

'Caro, your father was charged by the police this morning. They took him away and he won't be coming home. He's going to prison.'

I start to tremble. What she is saying makes no sense.

'You father has been drugging me with sleeping pills and tranquilizers.'

'Hang on, Mum – what are you saying?'

'There's more. Your father invited men to the house while I was unconscious in the bedroom. I've seen photos. I'm asleep, lying on the bed on my front, and there are men doing things to me. Men I've never seen before – different ones each time.'

I lose control. I start shouting, insulting my father. I want to break something – anything I can; everything, if possible.

'Caro, I'm telling you the truth. I had to look at the photos for the police. My heart almost stopped there and then. The lieutenant told me that there were videos too – lots of them – of the abuse. He asked me to look at one, but I couldn't. Even a photo was almost too much for me. The lieutenant understood. He said: "I'm so sorry. What your husband has done is monstrous."'

She breaks down in tears.

Pierre hugs me.

In my mind, images appear, merging into each other, each more appalling than the next: Mum lying on her bed, her eyes closed, her body paralysed, an unknown man looming over her…

> I can still see you behind the steering wheel of your black Renault 25, stuffed with bags and cases as we set off on holiday. You told jokes, put on Barry White and sung along, your head swaying along with the beat, just as excited as us, the kids in the back seat. A happy memory that has just shattered, replaced by the image of a man who conducts secret orgies and lives a constant lie. When Mum tells me about your last breakfast together, what lingers is the fact that it was so ordinary. What depths of dishonesty does it take to have maintained, all these years, the tranquil illusion that everything was normal?

Mum hangs up. She has other calls to make – first David, my elder brother, and then Florian, the youngest of her three children.

I collapse. Crushed by what I've heard, I cling to my husband. I can barely breathe.

My father drugged my mother and served her up to strangers to be raped. It should not be possible to string such words together, for the sentence that they form to make any sense. The very idea is so steeped in violence it is almost impossible to contemplate – like a knife so sharp that the gleam of the blade blinds you, its edge so keen that you don't immediately realise how deep it cuts. What if Mum had overdosed? What if she had never woken up? Almost eight years have gone by since Mum retired and they moved to the rural backwaters of Provence. Eight years of unending horror.

And I was blind to it all. I suspected nothing. Neither did she. There was not even the slightest hint of what was going on.

The drugs my father slipped her – timed and dosed with precision – turned my mum into a blank slate. I think back to the phone calls when she had seemed so distracted, lost in her mind. We – her three children, all of us living 700 kilometres away – began to worry. What else could it be, but the onset of Alzheimer's? My father pooh-poohed us. He would say: 'You know your mother; she has no idea how to pace herself, she's always on the go. She manages her stress by rushing from one thing to the next.'

In 2017, we talked Mum into an appointment with a neurologist in Carpentras, the nearest big town. He talked about transient global amnesia – a sort of black hole that opens up momentarily, drawing in all memories, only to vanish as mysteriously as it came. A transient state that does no lasting damage. What we didn't realise – although if we'd thought to ask, any specialist could have confirmed it – was that this kind of thing never happens several times in a row.

In late 2018, my uncle, a retired GP, suggested some kind of balancing mechanism was at play: He told her: 'You're like a vacuum cleaner whose bag is full. It can't suck in any more so it stops working to avoid burning out. When you've had too much, you disconnect and that way you recover your strength, ready to bounce back.' We were all convinced he was right. Mum had a brain scan done all the same, but of course it revealed nothing. Needless to say, it never occurred to us to ask for a drug test.

But Mum got more and more anxious as time went by, and the episodes of amnesia piled up. She couldn't sleep, began to lose her hair and her weight plummeted – ten kilos dropped off her in less than eight years. She was haunted by the thought that she might have a stroke out of the blue, particularly when she took the long train journey to visit me in Paris or found herself in charge of looking after her grandchildren.

Worried about the potential risk she might pose, she gradually stopped driving. Little by little, she was losing her autonomy.

In 2019, she tried another neurologist, this time in Cavaillon, another sizeable town in the region. He told her she was simply prone to anxiety. He prescribed melatonin to help her sleep more soundly…

I have to go to her. I can't leave her isolated in a distant corner of the country, all alone in the house that was the scene of such atrocities.

Pierre steps up. Of course I have to go. He'll take charge, make it happen.

I have to get outside. I have to call my brothers. When David picks up, I can tell by the tone of his voice that he still doesn't know. I beat Mum to him, and I instantly regret it, but I can't hold back now.

David listens in silence. Afterwards, it takes him ten seconds to digest what he has heard and find his voice.

'Come on – this can't be true. Caro, is this your idea of a joke?'

He interrogates me, but I don't have all the answers. I wish I was able to lead him to a calmer place, because I can sense him backing away. He hangs up, intent on calling Mum.

When I finally reach Florian, the youngest of us, he has already heard from my mother. He's in shock.

'How could he do such a thing to Mum? And to us? Did he ever think about us?'

Like a child, all I can do is cry.

Thinking back to an episode during the summer of 2018, Florian's anger wells up. With his wife and his two daughters he had spent several days at our parents' house. During their last dinner together, the evening before they left, they witnessed a scene that made a deep impression. Mere minutes after sitting down to eat, Mum seemed to disconnect from her body. Her elbow suddenly slid off the table and she nearly fell off her chair, as if she were dead drunk. Drained of energy in an instant, she collapsed like a rag doll.

'I still don't know how to describe what we saw, Caro. It was like her strings had been cut. We tried to talk to her, but it was like talking to someone who had been hypnotised. She just sagged where she sat. Her eyes were empty. She didn't react to anything we said.'

My father took her off to bed. 'It's for the best. This happens to her from time to time – she burns the candle at both ends and then has to switch off for a while.'

The truth, of course, was that he had snuck into a back room and slipped a cocktail of drugs into her aperitif before we sat down to dinner. The dose was beginning to take effect.

But that evening my father insisted that Florian and his family were the cause, having worn her out. They had no option but to get into their car and leave.

When I hang up, I have to walk around the neighbourhood twice to get a grip on myself.

It's a chilly evening, but anger consumes me. Pierre comes to get me.

He's the one who convinces my brothers to join me on the first train south the next day. With his words, he shakes them out of their dejection: 'You've got to pick yourselves up. Your mother needs you – all three of you.'

He doesn't stop there: 'More than that, you all need each other. You have to come together. None of you will make it through this if you try to stand alone.'

He's lucid too: 'You're going to need all your strength and all your courage. This is just the beginning. There'll be more to face – things that have yet to come to light.'

I contact my employers and tell them I'll be taking some days off. It's late. Time to try to get some sleep. But I can't be alone. When I finally drift off, my husband is by my side and my son's hand gripped in mine.

Tuesday, 3rd November 2020

When I wake up, my entire body aches and I have a stabbing pain in my back. My muscles are as sore as if I'd spent the night in a boxing ring. I throw some things into a bag, packing lightly even though I have no idea how long I'll be away.

I drop Tom off at school, telling him for the third time that I'm going to visit his gran down south and that I'll bring her back home with me. At the school gate I pull him into a hug, drawing in his scent. I feel the wonder of him – his fine neck, his tiny ears, his wavy hair, his nose, the little furnace of his cheeks burning against mine. I want to embed the sensation of him inside me, to always have it with me. He's my secret charm, the nugget of gold I keep hidden in my heart.

Tom looks up at me. Placing a hand on each side of my face to fix his eyes on mine, he tells me:

'Mum, you know how much I love you? Well, tell Gran that I love her just as much.'

I file away his words, and his unique way of stroking my cheeks, as treasured memories. Why I don't know, but it didn't occur to him to mention his grandfather.

As I make my way to the station to catch my high-speed train, I decide to call the police lieutenant. When he picks up, he's not surprised to hear from me.

I tell him that we – my brothers and I – would like to talk to him as soon as we get off the train in Avignon. He tells me he can't give us much time because there's a legal limit on the time they have to prepare the charges against our father.

They have to submit their case to the criminal court in Avignon within 48 hours of taking my father into custody. They don't have a moment to lose. They still have to go through my parents' house to find physical proof of the chemical submission inflicted on my mother.

I hang up, close my eyes and recite the facts to myself: my father drugged my mother so that a bunch of strangers could rape her. For eight long years. As I silently voice the words, I sense their full meaning. I might still be standing, but inside I collapse.

* * *

Platform four of the Massy TGV station outside Paris.

'The 9.25am train for Marseille is about to arrive.'

I turn to Pierre, beside me on the platform, unaware of what I'm about to say: 'I'm scared.'

He puts his arms around me and holds me tight. If only time could stop and we could stay like that, my head on his shoulder.

When I reach my seat, I look through the window. My husband is still there, on the platform. For the first time, I notice the depth of sadness in his eyes.

Never again will he see the country house in Provence that held such marvellous, tender memories for both of us.

> You light the charcoal on your beloved barbecue and lay out the skewered meat, looking up to smile at me. The sun bounces off the walls of the house, embracing us all in its heat. Tom is on the swing, Pierre busying himself with the wine. A summer patio and a happy family. I hate you.
>
> Were you always so twisted? Were we always so blind? Can you fail to see your own father? Who are you, for real?

I need to escape. I put in my earbuds and let my phone choose some music at random. It comes up with Fleetwood

Mac's 'Dreams', taking me back to my childhood. No escape there. The song reminds me of a paradise I thought would last forever.

In the toilets, my reflection is haggard. Even the obligatory mask doesn't hide the fact that I seem to have aged ten years in the space of twenty-four hours. I can't stop thinking of Mum. He made her into a sexual object, a toy, a possession and we failed to protect her. Yet we saw her so often. She would come to Paris and spend weeks with me, or my brothers Florian and David. We are all really close, and her six grandchildren adore her as much as she does them.

Every time she returned home from Paris to her house in distant Mazan, she would fall off the radar for 48 hours. If we called her, it was my father who picked up. He would say she was resting, recovering from her stay with us. She was getting too old to cope with the hectic pace of life in Paris. The same old lie. The lie we fell for time and again. As did she. He kept on at her, insisting that the gentle rhythm and balmy air of Provence were better for her. That she couldn't cope with Paris. She heard this so often that she began to believe it herself.

I lost count of the number of times I tried talking to her, only to find her completely adrift. That she couldn't recall conversations we had shared just a day or two before disturbed me. It was as if her brain was continually being reset.

One day, in mid-April 2019, Tom asked to call his gran, who'd just left us to go home. He'd been in a rugby tournament and wanted to tell her all about it. As soon as she picked up, she started repeating herself like a broken record, uttering phrases that made no sense. I could see from Tom's face that something was wrong and took the phone from him.

'Mum, what day is it?'

She couldn't tell me.

I called my father to tell him that something was wrong with Mum, that I was worried about her health, and that we had to find out whatever was causing her to act this way. He just changed the subject. Over ten years, he did so over and over again, always finding an excuse to fob off my questions. Had we thought about it, we might have noticed that her moments of absence happened only when she was back home with my father, and never when staying with my brothers or myself. If only we had thought about it.

> Thinking back, you were always a bit slippery. You create one company after another, but they always go bust, leaving you holding the bag. You're always up to something dodgy – going into business with a crooked

partner or divorcing Mum for so-called financial reasons, supposedly to benefit us, then remarrying her years later. You create uncertainty and duck any problems that come up. What on earth are you telling the investigators? Are you inventing excuses, trying to lead them astray, or have you owned up? If so, then for the first time in your life you're not wallowing in self-pity.

Mum never liked taking medicine. If she had to take paracetamol, she took the smallest possible dose. She has never smoked, she's a huge walker and she's never been addicted to anything. The only vice she ever had was chocolate, and that was back before she retired.

Her most recent episode of memory loss was on the 22nd October. Twelve days ago.

One of her friends who lived outside Paris talked to her on the phone around five in the evening. The next day, she left her a voicemail: she had been disturbed by mother's state during the call and wanted to know if something was up, something she should be aware of.

When my mother heard this message, she was utterly perplexed. She had no recollection of having talked to her friend the previous day. Shaken, she brought it up with my father. He pretended to have no idea what she was talking about.

I make it back to my two brothers. We huddle together in our corner of the train, not letting each other go. The other passengers keep glancing at us.

By 1pm, we're in Avignon. It takes us a quarter of an hour to find our way out of the station to the taxi rank, despite the fact that all three of us know the place by heart. We take a different exit from the one where our father used to greet us.

> You open your arms wide, Tom jumps up into them, and you smile. The same you who smuggles drugs into Mum's glass, posts ads online and captures on video the horrors that ensue.

We reach Carpentras. Mum is there, waiting for us in front of the main police station. She looks utterly lost, a mere five feet four inches tall in clothes that look too big for her, her hands hidden away in the pockets of her puffy mauve jacket.

Even her white mask seems oversized, obscuring her face, puffy from tears. Dark circles surround her distinctive black eyes. She's unsteady on her feet, teetering visibly from side to side.

I leap out the taxi and rush to her, pulling her into a hug. My brothers do the same. She almost breaks down. I take her hand, mothering my mother.

We enter the police station. In the main hall with its yellow and beige walls, I realise that my father must be there too, shut up in a nearby cell. Could we see him? Speak to him? Out of the question – a suspect detained for this kind of crime is held in isolation for as long as it takes.

One of the officers in charge of the enquiry takes us to a tiny office into which a table and two chairs have been squeezed. Mum says she'll wait outside in the corridor.

I can't stop thinking about my father. Was he interrogated in this very room?

The officer invites us to sit down. My brothers prefer to stand. I glance at them. Florian gives the officer a sombre look, something I've never seen him do. David is doing his best to look normal and at ease, if only on the surface.

The room is so tight I feel like we've all been lured into a trap. If the walls had started to move, crushing us all, I wouldn't have been surprised.

The officer runs through the enquiry's conclusions. We turn deathly white.

'For the last eight years, if not longer, your father has been drugging and raping your mother on a regular basis. He filmed it all and posted the images on the internet.'

Just listening to it leaves us feeling soiled.

'In September 2013, he started reaching out to others through an online sex site, inviting at least 53 different men to come to the house and rape your mother while she was unconscious. He distributed photos of her to draw them in and talked openly about what he was doing on a series of online forums. No money ever changed hands.'

A final, perverse twist: my father, who was always short of money, didn't try to profit from his abuse of Mum. His sole motive was the pleasure it gave him.

Later, we discover that he subdued her with a mixture of lorazepam, a benzodiazepine used to treat anxiety, sold in France under the name Temesta, and zolpidem, a powerful sleeping pill only prescribed for severe, but short-term, insomnia. Year after year, my mother's body was polluted by massive doses of these chemicals.

That very morning, the officer had taken a team to search the house, this time while my mother was present. My father had concealed the drugs in a tennis sock stuffed into a hiking boot hidden away in the garage. He admitted everything when being interrogated a few hours before we got off the train.

The search also revealed the most recent prescription he'd obtained – a repeat prescription, signed off by one of the village doctors. Given how many boxes of pills my father had been given over the years I can't help wondering whether the doctor might have been an accomplice.

The officer tells us that our father faces a list of potential charges, each expressed in stark legal jargon: 'Administering a substance capable of altering the victim's judgement or depriving the victim of free will in order to commit rape or another act of sexual assault; invasion of privacy by taking and distributing sexual images; sexual assault compounded by administering, without consent, a substance capable of altering the victim's judgement or depriving the victim of free will; facilitating rape by others with several aggravating factors; acts of voyeurism with several aggravating factors; rape with several aggravating factors.'

That's when I ask the officer if my father has expressed any regret, whether with regard to my mother or to us, his children.

'No. The nearest he's come was when he thanked me for – and I'm quoting here – lifting a weight off his chest.'

Words fail me. Florian recoils, his jaw tight as a vice. David tries not to react, relying on the support of the wall behind him, hiding his hands deep inside his pockets. I'll never forget how ghostly white he became, how frozen, how horror-struck. As for me, I had no idea if I would be able to sit through the rest of the interview.

The officer ploughs on.

'Your father came to our attention for the first time on the 12th September 2020 on suspicion of having filmed up the skirts of three women shopping in a supermarket in

Carpentras. Each of them chose to press charges, leading to him being taken in for questioning.'

Silently, I give thanks to these three women. If they hadn't pressed charges, who knows how many more rapes would have been committed as the country dipped in and out of lockdown. Unbeknownst to themselves, these women saved my mum. It takes courage and determination to walk into a police station and report a sexual assault, and they possessed both. Without them, the police would never have discovered the contents of my father's telephone.

When the police technicians finally deciphered the hard disk he kept at home, they unearthed over 20,000 pornographic photos and videos. These images went way beyond the realm of sexual fantasy. It was a gallery of barbaric acts.

At that point in time, I knew nothing about the use of drugs as a means of subjecting others. I'd heard tell of GHB, the date-rape drug, but had no idea how widespread its use had become. Nor did I know that rapists were turning more and more towards sleeping pills and anti-anxiety medicine, substances without colour or odour and easy to dissolve in a drink.

My ignorance strikes me as almost culpable. I had thought I was intuitive, quick to catch on to what was really happening around me. In truth, I had been blind to it all.

Not so the police investigation team working out of Carpentras. They had thrown themselves into the case when they first arrested my father for upskirting back in September. Discovering the horrors on his phone, they then worked in a race against the clock to save my mother from her torturer. Their investment and commitment paid off. In less than two months, they had analysed most of the horrific videos and found and identified 53 of the aggressors, otherwise anonymous men who had appeared out of nowhere in my mother's bedroom. Their work could not have been more exemplary.

When the officer has finished telling us everything and freed us from that tiny room, I ask him to pass a message to my father before he is taken before a judge and sent into custody: 'Tell him I will never forgive him for ruining our lives.'

Reunited with Mum, we sit with her as she goes through a final formality – rereading and signing the definitive version of her statement. We read alongside her, stunned by the things we discover. Our father was constantly taking blood tests, including one for AIDS in March 2020. His prescription history – obtained from the state health insurance records – reveals him to have been a regular consumer of Viagra. I suddenly realise that he had exposed my mother to a host of potential sexually transmitted diseases. He offered his wife up to all and sundry, men of whom he knew nothing, and never required them to wear a condom. Worse, there was proof that he had, on occasion, forbidden them to do so.

Once again, my head spins. No wonder my mum had had so many gynaecological problems over the past years – ones that we stupidly put down to her so-called chronic fatigue. It's clear we will have to take her for a whole series of tests, from which we can only fear the worse. AIDS? Hepatitis? Other infections? I try to mark this down mentally as an urgent requirement, hoping it won't get lost amongst all the other information we are having so much difficulty absorbing.

Although the police had organised a short session for my mother with an in-house psychologist, no other medical follow-up has been offered. We have to take charge. Luckily, I have a cousin who is a GP, but I can't help wondering who steps in to help those in similar circumstances who don't have a personal connection to a doctor.

Before he leaves us, the offer informs us that our father had made an official request to be fitted with a monitoring device and released from custody. I make very clear what I think of such an idea, and of my father for even daring to suggest it.

When we leave the police station, we head immediately

to the nearby courthouse. We have to fill out a dossier to request legal aid. Our mum needs a lawyer to stand up for her in court.

We don't make it back to my parent's house until four in the afternoon. As the automatic gate to the driveway opens, their French bulldog – a loyal companion to my father – lunges out, barking.

> When you pulled into the house in the car, you always opened the door so that the dog could leap in and sit proudly on your knees. You never skipped this little ritual. Clearly you felt the dog deserved better treatment than the rest of us.

I enter the house, draw in the familiar smells, drop off my bag in the room with the violet colour scheme where I always slept with my husband and son, walk past the family photos in the corridors, glance at my father's paintings, one of them a female nude. Each step is like a station of the cross. All of my memories of this place – once so comforting, so joyful – are tainted now. The walls around me are silent witnesses of the abominable scenes that took place over the years. Everywhere I look, I see the shadows of my father's dark side. A family photo, full of smiles and joy, now strikes me simply as proof of the manipulation and dishonesty that went on for so long. As for his paintings, my urge is to burn them all, starting with the nude portrait.

Taking a deep breath, I join my mother in the kitchen. My brothers have taken a decision: we will all be out of this place within three days, less if possible. They go to work in the lounge, where my father's desk is a lurking presence. The footprint of his computer – now in the hands of the police – is clearly visible. He spent most of his free time glued to it, particularly in the evening, and sometimes long into the night. Immobile on his chair, puffing on an e-cigarette, his attention never wavered from the screen. Not even when the house was overrun by his children and grandchildren.

We have to pack as much as we can, because we will never let our mother live alone in this house ever again.

My parents thought that this would be the perfect haven for their retirement. My father, a passionate cyclist, adored the many bike routes that ran through the surrounding countryside. My mother prized everything about the region. She loved nearby Mont Ventoux, the scrub-filled landscapes that ran to the horizon, the neighbouring villages and their summer festivals, quirky shops and market gardens. She even felt a certain fondness for the icy Mistral winds that winter brought.

Sitting in a quiet and well-maintained cul-de-sac, with just enough neighbours to give a sense of community, their house was a haven for family and friends. Beyond its ideal size and convenient layout, it was full of charm. It had pale blue shutters, a sheltered garden with a suntrap corner, a pool just deep enough for my mother, extensive flower beds that my father fussed over obsessively, a gravel walkway lined with elegant lights, a wide-spreading mulberry tree, tall pink laurels, and an olive tree that we had given them to mark Tom's birth. Throughout their years of living there, they had moulded their home in their own image.

The patio, where the house met the garden, was my favourite spot. It was the scene of our barbecues, our endless discussions, our playful laughter, our sunset drinks, our noisy games of Trivial Pursuit and Money Drop, and our al fresco dinners, where the food often gave way to evenings of music and dance.

For my son, my husband and I, it was our happy place. I had always assumed the same was true for my parents.

My phone drags me back to the present moment. A local number, not anyone I know. Expecting the worst, I answer. It's the police officer we've just been with. He asks me to return to the station so that he can give me back some of the digital equipment they had confiscated. He says some of the USB sticks they took have no bearing on the enquiry. I glance at the clock on the kitchen microwave: 5:25pm.

I can't help feeling that he's holding something back.

And that, whatever it is, it can't be good. I try to turn the time to my advantage. As casually as I can, I ask if I couldn't pick everything up the next day, given how late it is.

But no, my instinct was right. He tells me he has something he needs to show me, something that concerns me directly. Trembling, I end the call and mechanically pick up the car keys and my handbag. I'm heading out when Florian says he'll drive me to the station, insisting there's no way he'll let me go without him by my side.

Both of us are convinced that a terrible revelation is yet to come. En route to the station, my heart beats so fast my chest seems ready to explode. A burning sensation spreads across my back. I wind down the car window, sucking in the fresh air.

The 20 minutes it takes us to get to Carpentras feel like an eternity. I enter the station convinced that I will leave it feeling utterly demolished. My brother steers me in. Just as well, as I can't feel my legs.

It's after 6pm, but there are still members of the public and plenty of uniforms in what is supposed to be a quiet provincial police station. I feel jealous of those who are there to report a snatched handbag or a break-in.

An officer calls me forward. Florian gets up to accompany me, but he's told he can't. He has to stay where he is. Ten paces take me into a room, just as small as the previous one, where two officers sit behind their computers. I take a seat, slip my hands down onto my thighs and slowly squeeze them, hoping to distract myself from the anxiety that threatens to choke me.

A large blue folder lies on the table. Photos printed on sheets of A4 poke out from it.

I'm afraid of what I'm about to discover.

One of the officers tries to calm me. 'You can handle this', he tells me. I only have to look at two photos. All they want to know is if I'm in either of them.

The first picture shows a young woman with dark brown hair and a straight-cut fringe lying on a bed on her left side. It's nighttime, with a bedside lamp lighting the scene. She's wearing a thick white pyjama top and beige underwear.

She's asleep, but the quilt covering her has been lifted aside to expose her buttocks. She's deathly pale, with dark-ringed eyes.

I look up at the officer and tell him I'm not sure whether or not it's me.

My phone vibrates in my pocket. It's David, no doubt impatient to know what's happening. I can't answer him and leave it to vibrate. It takes him a long time to give up.

The officer hands over the second photo. The bedsheets seem familiar, but I can't be sure. The pose is the same as the previous image. Not just similar, identical. Creepily so.

It's the same young woman too and it makes me recoil in exactly the same way.

It was taken in a different room. The woman is wearing a black-and-white patterned sleeveless sweater. The underwear hasn't changed, though. I ask to look at the first photo again. Definitely the same underwear. But, once again, I tell them I don't think it's me.

The officer studies my face for a brief moment.

'I hope you don't mind me pointing this out, but don't you have a brown mole on your right cheek, just like the young woman in the photos?'

I force my eyes back to the images, and finally the veil drops from my eyes. I start to shiver, my vision is disturbed by a host of tiny starbursts, my ears start ringing and I jerk back in the chair. The officer calls in my brother. Florian kneels before me, holds my hands, and tells me to try to breathe along with him.

Someone finally thinks to fetch me a glass of sugar water.

How did he manage to take my photo in the middle of the night without waking me up? Where did the underwear come from, as I'm sure it's not mine? Did he drug me? Did he go beyond the photos? Did he – I can't keep the unthinkable at bay – abuse me?

It takes some time for me to be able to look directly at the police officers and admit that it is indeed me in the photos.

I try to think when they might have been taken. It's hard to say, but they don't look recent.

One of the officers, perhaps trying to reassure me, says: 'Your father underwent a psychiatric evaluation in September 2020, when he was first brought in, and it showed a marked proclivity for voyeurism.' He goes on to say that the elements they have gathered suggest that my father's sexual obsessions grew stronger over time. That as the years passed, he sank deeper and deeper, until he crossed the line into his unspeakable treatment of my mother.

Florian asks if he can see the pictures of me. I think he should, because otherwise he might cling to the idea that my father could not possibly have done something so unthinkable.

Now we're both in a state of shock. Several minutes go past.

The next step can't be avoided. I have to file a complaint against my father. I have to step up and join the other victims. If I don't, what he did to me cannot be held against him. It's only two photos, but they, too, must be weighed in the balance, as additional proof of his perversity.

'Have these jogged your memory in any way? Brought even the tiniest fragment of the past to the surface?' asks the officer.

For no conscious reason, I think of Pascale, my mother's

best friend. We haven't seen her for over 20 years. They met in work, in the early 1980s. My mother, who was ten years older than Pascale, treated her like her little sister. She became part of the family and was chosen to be Florian's godmother. Pascale had been present on many important occasions. She was always popping round to the house, and was always made to feel at home.

Yet in the early 2000s, there was a falling out, for reasons I had never quite understood. I knew that my father had played a key role in the breakup. Right from the start of their friendship, he was always criticising her, trying to drive a wedge between her and my mother.

One day, at work, Pascale had warned Mum that my father had done something she couldn't keep to herself. He had propositioned her.

'You have no idea who you're living with. You've got to open your eyes. Your husband isn't the man you've always taken him to be.'

My mother flew off the rails, telling her to get out of her office.

My father denied everything when my mother confronted him. He even threatened to seek out Pascale and beat her up for what she had said. Mum and Pascale never spoke again. At the time, my father's reaction left me puzzled. It seemed so out of proportion for someone who was supposedly beyond reproach. It nagged at me for a long time.

The end of their 20-year friendship broke my mum's heart. But my father insisted that the end had to be final and so it became.

I'm now convinced that this was the first step in my father's campaign to turn my mother into his puppet.

> You could make her laugh so easily. Any old joke you told would start her off. I thought it a miracle that after all these years living together, you still found so much to laugh about. Your early years in the house in Provence were so joyful. Everything brought a smile to your lips.

I tell the officer he should contact Pascale. I read my statement over and sign it. We get up, ready to go. I tell myself to keep my imagination in check, to avoid speculating about what else might have happened beyond the two snapshots my father had taken of me.

Florian and I hurry down the stairs, putting as much distance as we can between ourselves and the photos, as if we were running from a monster, hoping to outpace it, to leave it shut up in that room in the police station, to save ourselves from its claws.

Heading back to the house, I call David and tell him everything. Another gut punch.

I can't get over the position I'm in on the photos. It just didn't look natural to me. I'm a light sleeper, prone to waking at the slightest disturbance. Drugs alone could have made such a pose possible.

I find my mother in the lounge, facing down an array of documents spread out before her – unpaid bills, outstanding debts, accounts in the red. My father had hidden them away in a series of plastic folders.

She looks up casually, as if I'd just come back from a pleasant walk. Although I'm not sure she's capable of taking it in, I feel obliged to tell her about the photos. When I do, I'm not surprised when she doesn't react. She just stands there, a blank look on her face.

'Are you absolutely sure it's you?'

She doesn't believe me. I feel sick. Maybe her doubt is an unconscious attempt to shield herself, but it hurts me all the same. Florian steps up and insists that the photos are of me. His tone is firm, definitive. He adds that he's sure he recognised the background in one of them. It was a room in my parents' old apartment. Which would mean it was taken long before 2013.

Mum remains in denial.

Suffocating, I need to get some fresh air and talk to Pierre.

Right now, he's my oxygen. I go outside to the patio and call my husband.

He's furious and wants me to get a lawyer. He's looked into it and thinks there's only one choice – someone who has built her reputation on challenging cases, known for fighting ferociously for her clients. I tap in her number as I walk back into the lounge. My mother, though still in the room, is clearly absent, murmuring that everything is moving too quickly for her to keep up.

The lawyer answers. She immediately insists that we'll need toxicology and psychiatric reports. She brushes aside my financial fears. Yes, the case will involve a lot of expenses, but the financial damages that will undoubtedly be awarded to my mother when the case is resolved will cover them. She tells us we must write to the investigating magistrate and exactly what to say. Even in my state of shock, I understand what is implied by our exchange. We're about to undertake a marathon, a long battle that must play out through the judicial system. None of us will be spared. Grief and loss await us all. My mother will have to let her husband go; we will lose our father.

'In this kind of case, it takes at least three years to get to a final court judgement,' the lawyer tells me. 'The law moves at a glacial pace, despite the fact that victims suffer with each passing day.'

The lawyer's language will become my own, wrenching me from the everyday world and into to the parallel universe of the legal system. A place where a soft landing is unheard of.

Eating still feels impossible. I manage to spoon down a little soup and resume going through the drawers of my father's desk. Stuffed randomly into folders I find fines for driving offences late at night on distant motorways, bill reminders and debt notifications. Where did all these debts come from? Why so many summons to a civil court in Carpentras? My mother can't answer my questions. Not just because she is exhausted, but because she delegated all administrative and financial matters to my father long ago. She didn't even handle the grocery shopping. My father insisted on doing it on his own, pretending it was for her sake. Aside from the odd walk with her friend Sylvie, my mother's social life had shrunk to almost nothing. I realise how far she had fallen under my father's control.

She explains that she never had access to the mail that poured into the house. My father insisted on gathering it up himself, and would pounce upon it as soon as the postman left. He would even push her back if she tried to help. Feeling marginalised, she gave up, accepting that this was part of his domain.

Even though I'm exhausted, I'm terrified by the thought of sleeping in the violet room that had welcomed me so often before. How many aggressors, intent on raping my mother, had passed through this house? I can't shake off the fear that one of them might come back in the middle of the night, until Florian brings his mattress and lays it down beside my bed.

Back home in Paris, Tom and Pierre are watching a football match between Paris Saint-Germain and Olympique Marseille. Tom and my father – his beloved Grandad – used to call each other before these matches and argue about how it would play out. This time round, my son turns to his father and says:

'Dad, will you tell Grandad I think Olympique Marseille's going to crush them?'

As the stadium yells and the players come onto the pitch, Pierre is grief-struck, knowing that Tom's pre-match ritual is lost forever. There's anger, too, that my father could do such a thing to Tom, who had placed his Grandad at the centre of his affections. The match over, Pierre sends a final text message to my father.

He knows that my father, stuck in a cell without his phone, can't read what he's typing. But he does it anyway. One last time.

> You'll never see this. But still …
>
> Watching Olympique Marseille play next to

your grandson means listening to him say, every five minutes, tell Grandad this or that.

But I'll never tell Grandad anything ever again. Neither will he.

What you've done is beyond contempt.

Depriving your grandson of the last grandfather left to him – beyond contempt.

It makes me cry. It makes me want to tell you to go to hell.

The two photos torment me all night long. I wake in the dark at 5:42am, having forgotten where I am. I can hear Florian's breathing. He's fast asleep, so close I could reach out and touch him. I want to go to the toilet, but am afraid to. The bathroom is down the corridor, near the front entrance. This house doesn't feel safe anymore. I make myself go, but I brace myself to take each step and light my way with my phone's torch, constantly checking all around me.

I rush back to bed and curl up under the sheets. I want to go back to sleep but I'm too tense. My ears prick up at the slightest sound.

Morning can't come too soon.

Wednesday, 4th November 2020

Two hours later, I wake to the sound of someone rummaging in a cutlery drawer. It's 7:45am. My mother is in the kitchen with a bowl of black coffee, her eyes fixed on the patio door. Maybe she's waiting for my father to come in from one of his early morning bike rides. She seems shrunken, sitting silently across from my father's empty chair. I'm so used to coming into the kitchen and finding them sharing breakfast, talking about the news or their plans for the day ahead.

I sit across from her. She pours me some coffee. It's the first time since my arrival that the two of us have been alone together. It's clear that her night was no more restful than mine.

Like me, she's been thinking of the photos she'd been

shown at the police station. Image after image of her, naked and unconscious. Her first reaction is to suspect them of being fakes – so disconnected from the long stretch of her married life that they ought to be unreal.

Mum starts talking about the morning of the 2nd November, when she and my father obeyed a joint summons to the police station. All my father's digital devices were already in police hands after his arrest in the supermarket in Carpentras. He had given her a watered-down version of that particular incident – two women, not three, had complained about him, and he said nothing about filming up their skirts – which he concluded by breaking down in tears and telling her he had done 'something really stupid'. My mother, who feared he was about to say he had some terrible illness, was almost relieved by his tale. All the more so when he swore to her that it was the first time he had done such a thing, that he had no idea why it had happened, and that it was just a moment of folly.

As performances go, this one was as pathetic as it was farcical.

He had told her after the Carpentras arrest that he was thinking of consulting a psychiatrist, just in case. Truth be told, he had no choice in the matter – it was one of the conditions imposed when the police had released him after questioning.

He added that he had decided to cancel a boating trip with his elder brother and nephew, originally set to start on the 30th September 2020, despite the fact that this month on a yacht on the high seas was something he'd really been looking forward to. His pretext was that he didn't want to leave her alone for so long, and that he'd had second thoughts about being cooped up with others in a cramped cabin. The reality was that he knew the police would soon want to speak to him again, and that he was forbidden to leave the country.

On the 13th October, a police officer in Carpentras contacted my mum, almost a month after my father told her about the 'something really stupid'. When the officer asked her if she was aware of an incident involving her husband in a Leclerc supermarket the previous month, she confirmed she was, not sounding particularly concerned, simply because what she thought she knew wasn't the truth. Fortunately, the officer insisted that she come along with her husband on the 2nd November. She said she would, blithely unaware of what awaited her.

Mum gets up to pour herself some more coffee. She tells me about her last moments with my father.

On the morning of the 2nd November, my father is astonishingly calm. They get up at the same time, around 7am, and take what she couldn't know will be their last breakfast together. My mother points out that it was the date her brother Michel was born, who had died several years before.

'Michel would have been 69 today.'

They leave the house at 8:45am.

My father wears bottle-green corduroy trousers and a pink Eden Park polo shirt that Pierre and I had given him. He adds a grey tracksuit top. My mother observes that the combination is not exactly elegant.

> 'Ah, your mother and her obsession with details,' you would sigh bitterly. I wrote off the acid tone as an inevitable consequence of 50 years spent together, unaware of the depth of the contempt behind your words. How much you must hate women and their concerns, given how you made your own wife pay for them all.

In the car, my father seems perfectly calm. He drives them to Carpentras without a hitch. Having found a parking space, he walks with complete assurance into the police station, like someone come to iron out a little paperwork.

A police officer asks my father to come with him. He gets up and, without a glance, leaves my mother behind. He's convinced he can worm his way out of the situation.

An hour later, my mother looks up and sees the same officer standing before her. This time he's come for her.

She thinks he's taking her to her husband, but the officer takes her into a room where there's just the two of them. She's surprised but doesn't dare ask why. Once she's answered the officer's question about what she thinks took place in the supermarket two months earlier, the interview takes a direction she didn't expect.

'Madame, how would you describe your husband's personality?'

'I'd say my husband was a good person, always attentive to others, always ready to give a hand. Everyone in our circle thinks highly of him. We met when we were both 18 and got married shortly after, in April 1973. We've three children and several grandchildren.'

'Would you say you've always got on well together?'

'Yes, I would. We've had a few rough patches, but we always got over them.'

'Do you have many friends locally? Ones you see often?'

'We moved to Mazan back in March 2013, so we've had plenty of time to build up a circle of friends. We meet up with them from time to time for lunch or dinner. We lead a very normal life, you know.'

'Do you take a lot of naps?'

Mum is thrown by the question. The ones that follow

unnerve her. How does she feel when she wakes up in the morning? How often does she have sex with her husband? Have they tried group sex or wife-swapping?

'Certainly not. I couldn't bear to have someone else touch me like that. For me, sex is about love,' she says, annoyed and alarmed. Surely they've got her mixed up with someone else?

The officer pulls out a folder, the first of many. With a mixture of embarrassment and pity, he tells her that the images she's about to see may shock her. Mum feels a stab of pain in her chest. She digs out her glasses.

On the first photo she is naked, clearly unconscious, lying on her stomach with a man behind her. The next three repeat the pose, but with a different man each time. She recognises her bedroom, her bed, her sheets, her lamps, her bedside tables, herself.

But she has no memory whatsoever of the acts captured by the camera.

She is shown a photo of my father kneeling next to the face of a naked woman – not her, and not anyone she knows. The woman is clearly unconscious.

The officer then says he has some videos he'd like to show her. She refuses to look at them, utterly thrown by what she's already seen.

That's when the officer tells her about my father's doping

strategy, how he would dissolve a mixture of sleeping pills and anti-anxiety medicine into her coffee or a glass of water, using doses that could knock her out for up to eight hours straight. Analysis of my father's digital devices – several SIM cards, a video camera, a normal camera, a hard disk with over 20,000 photos and videos – indicates that the acts of sexual violence started in September 2013. Fifty-three different abusers have been identified so far. They expect to unearth more as they keep on working the case.

'Everybody thinks rapes take place at night in an abandoned car park or a dark alley,' says the police officer. 'Truth is, in the majority of cases the aggressor is known to the victim – a partner, a relative, a friend or a colleague. Just as the use of drugs to facilitate rape happens far more often than everyone assumes. I'm not just talking about drugs being slipped into glasses in a night club. Chemical submission happens in domestic situations too, within couples.'

At best, Mum grasps half of what she hears, but that's more than enough to crush her. She's told she has to file a complaint against her husband. An urgent consultation with a psychologist will follow. When Mum finally gets home, her house is in a chaotic state. The police had carried out another search that morning, looking for additional evidence. They've carried away a computer my father picked up to tide him over while waiting the return of the one taken from his desk. All the drawers and cupboards have been gone through, their contents left in disorder. My mother, tight-lipped and exhausted, does what she can to tidy up the place.

She washes, dries and irons clothes for my father, packing them up to take to the police station so that he has something to change into. Her movements are robotic. Although her limbs move, her mind is elsewhere. From a psychological viewpoint, it's a classic case of dissociation – isolating a traumatic experience to make it easier to bear. Her defence mechanisms have kicked in.

By the time Mum wraps up her account of that unbearable day – including the part I already knew – I'm on my fifth coffee. My brothers join us in the kitchen.

We decide to clean everything out. I tackle the desk drawers, which clearly demonstrate that my parents' finances are as disorganised as they are dire I come across documents that talk of very substantial debts. And here was me thinking things could not get any worse.

David and Florian go through the other rooms. Our objective is to leave the house no later than tomorrow evening. None of us wishes to spend any longer than necessary under its roof.

Mum wants to keep as few things as possible from her life *before*. We take photos of most of the furniture and put them up for a quick sale online. We toss things into oversized bin bags and my brothers take them to the local dump. Only a few cardboard boxes containing souvenirs escape the cleanup.

> In your wedding photo – your second wedding, the final act of the farcical divorce that was supposed to have improved your financial situation – you're in a light grey suit, smiling, an arm around Mum. You look so solid, so confidant. A man to be trusted.

I remove his paintings and drawings from the walls, the fruits of his artistic endeavours since he and my mother settled down in this quiet village in Provence. One gets special treatment – the portrait of a naked woman. I grab it, take it out to the patio and smash it against one of the garden chairs.

It splits in two. As half of it twists in the wind I spot something written on the back in black pencil. A date – August 2016 – and a title. He'd called it 'Under My Thumb'.

That night I don't sleep a wink.

Today, my father was formally charged in the criminal court in Avignon, the regional capital. From there, he was sent to prison in nearby Le Pontet. He's being held in the wing reserved for sex offenders. Now, every time I say 'my father' I have to mentally add the words 'sexual delinquent'. The two photos taken of me continue to haunt me. What else didn't they show?

Thursday, 5th November 2020

My body is stiff. My back still hurts. My brothers have gone off to the dump. Today we leave, and there's still a lot to do before catching the train and taking Mum away with us.

My friend Anne calls to ask how I'm doing. She tells me not to wait any longer before consulting a psychologist and recommends one who specialises in dealing with trauma. I step out onto the patio and call the number she gave me.

I recount to the psychologist everything that my father did to my mother – the drugs, the rapes, the lies, the manipulation. Only afterwards do I mention the photos of me.

There is silence at the other end of the line. As I recount the obsessive anxiety that has gripped me for the past three days, I can't ignore the inconceivable damage done to me.

Before she lets me go, the psychologist tells me how much she costs, which is way beyond what I can afford. I remain sitting beneath the mulberry tree, the phone dead in my hand, long after the call is over. I can't get up.

I hear the gate open as my brothers return from their final trip to the dump. Florian comes over to me.

A flood of tears drowns my face.

'I think he drugged me. The way I'm sleeping in those photos – it's not natural. There's too much light – it would have woken me up. And I never sleep dressed like that, or in such a position. What else could account for the fact that the pose is identical on the two separate occasions? Then there's the underwear – it's identical too. Two photos taken in two different places at different times and yet so much matches. What other explanation can there be?'

Florian realises I'm having a panic attack. My psychological defence mechanism has gone off the rails. My brothers pick me up, carry me into the kitchen and put me in the recovery position, lying on my side on the tiled floor. I'm trembling and soaked in sweat. My mother watches, fear in her eyes. Florian is talking to me, but I can't hear him. I can't see straight either. Then, suddenly, the lights and sound cut out.

When I come to, there are firemen present. They take my blood pressure and give me some sugar water. One of them, a young woman with brown hair, speaks to me in a low, calm voice. I beg her to help me. I have only one thought: to flee as far as I can.

I manage to sit up for a few minutes. I hear talk about administering a sedative, which would mean taking me to the A and E in Carpentras.

David intervenes. If the firemen take me away in their ambulance, I'll never be able to leave with my brother and mother that evening. Since the thought of another day stuck in the house is intolerable, we tell them I'll go see a GP instead. Forty-five minutes later, my brothers help me into the office of the village doctor. He gives me a tiny pill and I instantly feel weightless. We return to the house, now just an empty shell. It's time to go. When we close the door behind us, my mother's face is clenched. She can walk out, but what happened here will stay with her forever.

Do you remember the party we held when you both reached 50, back in the house we all shared then – your children, your friends, the sumptuous food from the caterer, the superb wine, a soundtrack with all your favourites, the dancing that went on long into the night, you and Mum inseparable?

You made a speech, thanking her graciously for

all the happy years, calling her 'my one, my all' and ending with:

'Thank you, life, for giving me all this.'

When evening comes, we're standing on the platform in the train station in Avignon.

Thanks to Pierre, everything is ready when I bring Mum home with me. He's even added a few nice touches – a bouquet of flowers in the guest bedroom and a drawing Tom made especially for her, prominently displayed on the bookshelves.

Finally, some good news: Pierre says he has found the ideal psychologist for Mum. He's made an appointment for next Saturday.

It looks as if I might at last manage more than two hours' sleep tonight.

Friday, 6th November 2020

When I wake up, I can't speak. My voice has vanished, just like my life before.

Over breakfast, I take out the file of financial documents I brought with me from the house in Mazan. It takes me an hour and a half, going back and forth between bank statements and loan schedules, to get an overview of the situation. It's really bad.

The debts are huge. Mum can't tell me how they were being managed. She keeps repeating, 'He was in charge of all that.' I lose my patience.

'What on earth were you thinking, trusting him with your finances? He was always terrible with money! He proved it time and again – think of all the times he left the two of you in debt, struggling to dig yourselves out of a hole.'

She shrugs it off. I don't think she understands how far the perilous state of her finances will impact her standard of living.

I get on the phone to the banks. Things are as bad as I feared. Substantial loans were taken out, almost all of them in Mum's name.

They've already been pursued for missing payments on several occasions. The most recent judgement, notified by a bailiff from Carpentras, has them paying an annual penalty of 14% interest on a huge loan awaiting repayment since 2009. I add up everything she owes. I stare in despair at the total I've written down.

When my mother says not to worry, she'll take care of it, I can barely restrain myself trying to shake some sense into her. The more I learn about the way my parents lived, the more I realise how successfully my father had become her puppeteer and how meekly she had accepted it. Exhausted, I go and lie down. I see no way out of this nightmare.

I doze for a few hours. When I awake, my head is throbbing. It takes me a quarter of an hour to muster the strength to get out of bed.

Mum has been out for a walk. The short autumnal day is coming to an end. She seems relaxed, and I feel guilty about the way I scolded her. I promise to myself that I'll treat her more gently from now on.

Pierre nods towards the kitchen, slipping away and indicating that I should follow him discretely. I stiffen.

What is it this time?

He points to his laptop, open on the counter. I can tell he's nervous.

'Read that.'

It's an article from a news site called Actu17 that reports on criminal activity all over France. The headline screams at me: 'Carpentras – he drugged his wife, brought in strangers every night to rape her, and filmed it all!'

When my mother sees it she sags against Pierre, who has to carry her to the nearest sofa.

I can't protect her against this. An avalanche of similar articles online is inevitable. Pierre knows it too – it's his profession, after all. The regional press won't be far behind. I have to warn my brothers so that they're ready to face what's coming. Another blow, when we're still reeling from the first.

Florian is indignant. 'This is scandalous!'

We have no idea how to cope with this.

Who is this man who's been hiding inside my father for so long? I once had a father who looked out for me, took care of me. Where's he gone? Where's the man who walked me to school, encouraged me on the sports field, pushed me to study, helped me with my projects, talked me through my career choices? Where's the man who watched over and played with his grandchildren, basking in their love? How can you lead such a double life? How can you pull the wool over so many eyes for so many years?

Pierre comes up to me. I slap him. For the first time in our life. I've no idea what I'm doing. I've gone off the rails. My mother tells me to get a grip on myself. I don't even know where to start. My nerves are shattered. I lose control of my body as my muscles start to spasm. I cry out for help. Later on, Pierre will tell me that this moment – this hysterical outburst – left him terrified.

An ambulance pulls up. A neighbour, concerned, comes to the end of her driveway. She says something to me but I can't hear her. I'm not really there anymore.

In the hospital, I spend half the night on a stretcher in a corridor and the other in a bed. Twice, a doctor comes to see me. They should never have let me walk out of the police station in Carpentras, left to my own devices. If some kind of therapeutic support had been put in place it would have stopped me falling into this abyss, kept me out of this hospital. When will the justice system learn that a victim's need for support and protection doesn't stop when an arrest has been made and charges brought? How can we tell traumatised individuals to go back home as if all was well, particularly in cases of sexual assault?

Why haven't those in charge realised that the judicial system and the health system have to work hand-in-hand to ensure the safety of those who walk, trembling, out of a police station in the aftermath of a crime?

Saturday, 7th November 2020

I'm in an emergency psychiatric ward. A nurse asks me what caused my nervous breakdown the day before, as if it wasn't written in my face, in my bloodshot, tear-swollen eyes. I tell her, my voice wavering, barely audible, that I want to go home.

'I could cope with a normal hospital room, but not this, not a psychiatric ward.'

'It's up to you, but first of all tell me why they brought you here.'

I tell her. She recoils on her chair. I hear myself say: 'I know; it's the kind of thing that only happens in films.'

It hurts to talk about it. I can't stop crying. I desperately want to go home. The nurse tells me I'm suffering from emotional shock. Given my state, she can't just let me go.

I have to talk to a psychiatrist. She takes me into a room and gives me a phone to call Pierre. He picks up immediately.

'You're in a serious condition, Caro. It's a warning sign. You need help. You have to step back, look after yourself, try to rest.'

Two doctors come in. They suggest I take 'something to relax me' before the consultation.

I accept a pill. Minutes later, my body starts to slip away from me. As I tell them my story, my arms and legs grow heavier. I topple over onto my left side, unintentionally adopting the same position as the two photos taken by my father. I'm embarrassed and ill at ease. I apologise for not being able to sit up, but I can't fight it. The doctors say it would be better, given my utter exhaustion, if I stayed overnight. I hear and understand their words, but my eyes won't stay open. Is this what my mother felt?

When I wake up, the anxiety returns. Whatever the circumstances, losing control to a pill is an alarming experience. I can't place myself in space or time. I can't see my phone or my watch. My tongue feels like cardboard. I try to think straight, but feel my thoughts spin away from me. A nurse comes into the room and tells me I've been given an antipsychotic to help me relax and get some rest. Later on, I look up the drug they gave me – a treatment used in some cases of schizophrenia.

The nurse tells me: 'You're in a fragile state. Your nervous condition is too unstable for you to go home. You should spend at least one night here, under our care. Tomorrow morning, the duty doctor will review your situation.'

Hell, no. If I stay paralysed like this, my father will emerge from the shadows, scrutinise me, take photos, play with me like a toy, maybe even summon up other men. I'm not going to let it happen. I try to get up, but I'm caught in a trap, locked inside a body I don't control. I want my husband. 'I've called him,' says the nurse. 'He's going to come and drop off an overnight bag. We're going to put you on this wheelchair and take you into another room.' I'm wheeled into a steel cage, which turns out to be a lift. Fear grips me as I'm taken through corridor after corridor, an endless series of whitewashed walls. I hear screams, crying, protests. Scenes from *One Flew Over the Cuckoo's Nest*, with Jack Nicholson, run through my mind. Except this is no film.

I reach my room. My stomach hurts and tears pool in the hollow at the base of my neck. On a yellow pillow lies a white gown. I'm told to put it on.

Miraculously, Pierre appears in the doorway. The love I feel for him surges up and I want to run to him, to shout out his name, but I can't move and my throat, tightly choked, won't let any words out. He lays out pyjamas, a set of clean clothes and a toiletry bag. He tries to reassure me as best he can.

'It's just for one night, Caro. I've never seen you look so panicked. You've got me worried.'

I'm given a meal tray. I try the soup. It's disgusting. All I can swallow is a little water.

The night nurse brings me three pills, each a different colour, and tells me to take them straight away. For me, all they signal is danger.

I decide to only take one. Pierre watches over me as I slip into an artificial sleep. He gives me a kiss, tells me he loves me and quietly leaves the room.

I think of my mother, who has not come to see me.

At 2am I wake up, my mind foggy, still feeling the effects of the pill. Light seeps into the room from outside.

I have a raging thirst. The call switch doesn't seem to be working. I drag myself to the door. A short, solidly-built man comes up the corridor towards me, carrying a torch and a ring of keys.

'What are you doing up and about at this time of night?'

'I need a glass of water.'

For five minutes I try to talk to him, but he won't listen to me. He tells me I'm mad and pushes me back into my room, slamming the door shut. He may be a nurse, but he seems more like a prison guard to me. Which means I've been locked up with the insane. I have to get out of here. My sanity – quite literally – depends on it.

Sunday, 8th November 2020

A despairing cry heralds the dawn. From my room, I can hear a woman pouring out her pain and disarray. She keeps at it for over an hour, a liturgy of suffering in a language I don't understand. I can hear the sound of a metal bedframe slamming against a wall. I call for a nurse.

'We have to wait for a doctor to put her under. But don't worry, she's attached to her bed.'

I'm outraged. How can they leave people to suffer in this way, strapped to a bed? Having succeeded in getting hands on my phone, I call Pierre and beg him to come and get me. He reminds me that I have to be seen by the duty doctor first. That's who I have to convince to get home.

The doctor is a woman. She turns up late morning. She has a low voice and an inquisitive eye. She watches the way I move, evaluates the way I speak. Do I have suicidal thoughts? How do I feel about leaving the safety of the hospital?

'I want out. I know I need help, but I don't need this.'

She says she can prescribe drugs that would help me. I won't even consider it. I explain to her that the trauma I've suffered, that brought me to the ward, was a case of chemical submission. I'm not taking anything that can take control of me. That's what destroyed my world, after all.

The doctor insists on giving me a prescription for anti-depressants and sleeping pills. She tells me it's essential I have a psychiatric follow-up, and that it can't wait. I don't try to reason with her. I just nod my head. My only objective is to get out of this place.

Once she's left me on my own, I call my cousin the GP. She knows all about the drama we're caught up in.

'Take this from someone who loves you, Caro. You've had a terrible shock and you've kept going for several days in a state of profound psychological distress. It's time to ease up on yourself. You need a crutch, even if it's just a little one – believe me.'

She understands my reluctance to accept any drugs, and says she can prescribe some that carry no risk of addiction. She says I can use an antihistamine to calm myself if things get too stressful. She tells me how important it is to be alert to your emotional state, and anything that disturbs it, in the days immediately following a traumatic event.

I have every confidence in her. I love her like a sister, so I listen attentively to what she's telling me and then go on to give her the details of the sleeping pills the duty doctor prescribed.

She says I shouldn't hesitate to take one this evening. I've made up my mind – my cousin will be my doctor, at least for this first stage. How do women cope who aren't lucky enough to have a cousin like mine? If my experience – calamitous – of the medical support provided by the judicial system was representative, how can they possibly heal their wounds?

My next call is to Marion. A childhood friend, I need to hear her voice. Pierre has already told her about how I ended up in this hospital. She bowls me over with her empathy, both for my mother and myself. Both of us break down and we cry together for almost 20 minutes. When our voices return, I ask her to tell our close mutual friends what has happened, as I lack the strength to do so. Just as I lack the energy to call my two other childhood friends, even though they've stood by me for over 30 years.

When Pierre turns up, I'm ready to go. He finds me sitting on the bed staring out the window. I'm thinking about Mum. Why didn't she come to see me? Where is she?

'She went to stay with Florian. She left yesterday afternoon. Her psychologist told her – and she agrees – that the two of you are too fragile and that you shouldn't live together right now.'

I'm deeply hurt by her decision. I won't find my mother waiting for me at home. It feels like I have been abandoned. My eyes sting and I start to cry again.

Back home, I ache for my son, but he's out playing with a friend. He'll be home soon, but Pierre has arranged for him to go back later and stay overnight with his pal, so that I can sleep undisturbed.

I take a shower, washing off the scent of bleach from the hospital sheets.

Tom comes home, and the two of us go off for a walk, to get some air and let the wind scour us clean. I manage to clear my head for a short moment. Tom doesn't ask me any questions. He knows full well that I was in a hospital. All he says is that he would have preferred his Gran so stay with us. He misses her already. Me too, but I conceal my sadness and my resentment, and say nothing on the subject. We are inseparable for the rest of the afternoon. I read him some stories, watch him take his bath, and sit down to dinner with him and his father, even though I have no desire to put anything in my stomach. Then Pierre takes him off to his sleepover.

As soon as they're gone, my anxiety returns. I realise that Pierre will have to leave for work in the middle of the night, as he often does. I'll be left on my own. I feel vulnerable, like a child. Once again, I'm treading in my mother's recent footsteps.

At 9pm, I take an antihistamine. It has no effect. Or, rather, it is powerless against my terror at the notion that I might lose control and end up someone's prey. At 11:30pm Pierre comes to bed, and I'm still unable to doze off. He can tell I'm agitated. He's as worried as I am, but not for the same reasons – he's worried that I might be suicidal.

> You've made me fear sleeping alone, something that never worried me before. You've stolen my blissful sleep. The peace I once knew – you've crushed it underfoot.

I take another antihistamine around 1am. It takes its time to kick in, but I finally close my eyes. I'm vaguely conscious of Pierre getting up at 2am to go to work.

En route, at 3:18am, in the darkest hours of the night, he sends a text to my friend Mariam: 'SOS. Call me. Come ASAP. Please.' At 6:34am he sends another one: 'Caro's anxiety runs deep. She's wary of the medicine that's supposed to help her sleep, and it doesn't seem to be working.

I'm tortured by the thought that she's all alone while I'm in the office. I feel so guilty, but I couldn't get off tonight and I just assumed that she'd be able to sleep… If you call and get her voicemail, don't worry, it just means she's put her phone on flight mode. I left a note on the bedside table telling her to call me if she felt at all uneasy. Love.'

Around 4am I wake up soaked in sweat, as if my body wanted to expel everything I'd absorbed in the hospital. I'm still scared to find myself alone in bed. I might even be scared of myself – of the feelings that run through me, or the images that might rise up in my head.

I give myself a talking to, trying to hold my anxiety in check.

I finally get back to sleep at 6am, just as the first light of day begins to infiltrate the bedroom.

Monday, 9th November 2020

I open my eyes at 9am. As soon as I'm up, I feel like crying. I knock back one coffee after another. Around 10am, I do some housework just to keep myself busy. Repetitive tasks help to distract my body and brain.

For a while, I manage not to think. I don't hear Pierre come home, or Marion ring the doorbell. She rushes into the guest room where I'm tidying up. She catches me by surprise and I bury myself in her arms. Given what's happening she offers to stay with us. That way there'll always be someone there when I go to sleep, and I shouldn't feel so scared.

With her around, I feel more optimistic about the day ahead. But I still miss Mum.

A call comes through from my cousin. She has the results of my mother's initial blood tests. There's no sign of HIV or hepatitis C, but she tested positive for four different STDs. One of them is human papillomavirus, bringing with it the risk of uterine cancer. From now on, she'll have to undergo a test every year to check for any signs of cancer and treat them if necessary. A small burden to bear, compared with the hundred or so times she was raped over the last ten years. Since the most recent sexual assault was only weeks before – the 22nd October 2020 – she'll have to be tested again in three and then six months to be absolutely sure she's in the clear.

My cousin prescribes a course of antibiotics and regular gynaecological check-ups. She'll have to wait until the 19th December for a full forensic examination at a special clinic in Versailles. The results of the examination, an assessment of her general and gynaecological health, will be submitted as evidence in court.

You wake me up early in the summer to go cycling along the back roads of Provence. When faced with a tough incline, you egg me on: 'Keep at it, my girl! You can do it!' You beam with joy when you crest the ridge between the villages of Bédoin and Malaucène. I come up behind you and hop off my bike. We look around us, almost five hundred metres above sea level. The vista is amazing.

Marion looks after me over the next few days. There are so many things that I could do – cook a favourite dish, go for a run, read a book, watch a film, listen to music without breaking down in tears – but all that belonged to before. The Caroline who could do that was her father's daughter.

I insist on taking Tom to school in the morning. I know we have to have a talk.

Having lived inside a web of lies, I'm not going to do the same to my son. He has to know where his grandfather is. He'll find out soon enough, whatever I do. I know that his cousins, only a few years older than him, have found out. There's no point holding back.

Wednesday, 11th November 2020

Armistice Day. One of life's little ironies. My life is a battlefield and the two people who meant the most to me – my parents – are missing in action.

We're sitting on the sofa in the lounge. Tom's brown eyes are on mine. I have his full attention. His hands are folded together on his knees and he waits patiently for me to find the words.

'You know that things aren't going so well since we brought Gran home. You've probably noticed that I've been quite sad, even though I'm trying my best to get better. It's because of Grandad. He's done something very wrong. He's been telling lies and he's hurt Gran.'

'Hurt Gran? How did he hurt her?'

'He treated her badly. So badly, he broke the law.

And when you're mean and cruel to someone, then you have to be punished.'

'But Mum, I've never seen Grandad hurt Gran. I've never seen him hurt anyone!'

'I know, Tom. Neither had I. But he has, and that's why he's in prison.'

'What's a prison like?'

'It's a sad place. A big house with no garden. There are many floors and each has lots of tiny rooms. The rooms only have one window and the doors are always kept shut.'

'Can I visit Grandad in prison? Can I send him some drawings?'

'No.'

'But if you can't go see your father, you'll miss him. What are you going to do?'

'Right now, I'm very disappointed in him. And very angry. So angry, I don't want to hear from him. So, it's better that I can't see him.'

He doesn't understand. It's written on his face – sadness, uneasiness, resentment. It breaks my heart, but I keep a grip on myself. I mustn't cry. He looks up at me.

'I'd like to be on my own. Can I go to my room to think about it?'

I let him go and give him some time to himself – minutes, really, although they feel like an eternity to me – and then join him in his room. Tom lies on his back on his bed. His eyes, focused on the ceiling, are full of tears. He cries silently. Like a grown-up.

My anger against my father rises again. He's the one who inflicted this on Tom. I realise the extent to which an act of violence can spread beyond the initial victim, inflicting scars upon their entire family and beyond.

'Mum, I still don't get it. I've never seen Grandad be mean. I've definitely never seen him push Gran about. What you're saying – it can't be true. Someone's got it wrong,' says Tom in a broken voice through his tears.

I tell him we'll take him to see a doctor who's good at listening to kids.

I won't let your perversity become this family's curse. I won't let you hurt my son. I'll do everything to protect him from you. Your crime will not infect us, will not be transmitted from generation to generation. None of us will be like you – not my son, not my brothers. You should have been their example, a role model for them to follow. You've sacrificed us to your vices. You used us and tossed us aside. I despise you.

We're all stronger than you were. You made no attempt to extract yourself from the mud your father wallowed in. He was a piece of work – tall, intimidating, authoritarian. His hands looked like they would crush anything that fell into them. When I looked at Denis, my grandfather, in his jeans and biker jacket, with his single earring, I felt only shame. He didn't know what a conversation was – he had his opinions, and they were right, and the world had better just shut up and accept them. He had nothing but contempt for women, and seized every opportunity to put them down. For him, they were lesser beings, barely smart enough to do the housework. 'And let themselves be raped,' you would have added, no doubt.

When I was ten, your father made a cutting remark about my knees, saying they were ugly. His words upset me, but it was the way he looked at them that made me queasy.

While we're raking up the muck of your past, let's not forget what your twisted father did a few months after your mother died. He replaced her with Lucile – a young woman he and your mother had raised since she was a child. He took to his bed a vulnerable young woman who'd been under his care. Legally, it might not have been incest, but, in reality, what else could you call it?

You really are your father's son. The worst of him lives on in you.

Lucile was 30 years younger than Denis. She was a foster child. My grandparents, who were a foster family at the time, took her off the hands of Social Services when she was very young. She had developmental problems, probably because of the abuse and lack of affection she suffered at the hands of her birth family.

Denis took her as a substitute wife shortly after my grandmother's funeral. She took on all the domestic tasks in his house, and rarely left it other than to buy a packet of Gauloises for him at the village tobacconist or take his library books back.

My father, along with his brothers and sisters, initially opposed this relationship. But their mother's final words on her deathbed had been to tell them to obey and support their father, a man she had loved unconditionally. She had been utterly subjected to his will – a bad example, and a source of inspiration to my father.

He did nothing to prevent Denis drawing Lucile into his net, but he began to distance himself from his father and eventually stopped seeing him. An example I will follow, this time letting history repeat itself: my father broke off all contact with his father; I'm doing the same with mine.

Between the ages of seven and eleven – before their final break with him – my parents sent me to Chatillon-sur-Indre to spend part of the summer holidays with my grandfather and the young woman who had been his ward.

I still remember Lucille, who looked so much older than her 25 years, dressed in her drab housecoat. She could barely write, and wasn't allowed to change the channel on the television or the program on the radio without Denis's permission. She cleaned the house obsessively, folded sheets, and put the dishes away. David would imitate her behind her back, mocking the way she dusted furniture that was already spotless.

I had a soft spot for Lucille. She lived in a world of her own, cut off from people her own age, imprisoned by a man she had taken for a father, and who had then taken her for a wife. She spent her quiet moments on a swinging chair in the garden, staring at nothing and tearing out handfuls of hair. Many years would pass before I learned about trichotillomania, a compulsive mental disorder that manifests itself in this way.

I've never understood why my parents sent me to him, even with David as a source of solace and protection. When I reached 11 and my mother finally asked me if I was happy to go back for another few weeks one summer, I immediately said no.

Denis died in 2004. I've never missed him.

One day, when I was 40, I learned that Lucile had been

admitted to a psychiatric hospital. She was suffering from episodes of delirium and hallucinations. The news brought back a host of childhood memories. Denis would force her to take driving lessons in his beige Citroën C15. Sitting in the backseat, I witnessed the way he humiliated her, berating her impatiently until she broke down in tears. The more I remembered, the more I questioned why my parents had inflicted these holiday stays upon me. And why they had made no attempt to save Lucile from her fate.

> Ever naive, for the longest time I thought you'd escaped your disastrous family heritage. The truth was, alas, more straightforward: you never had it in you to confront your father; you've always been a self-centred coward. If you'd had the slightest courage, you would have saved Mum. And the entire family with her.

The next few days are hard. I feel like I've been imprisoned in my home, despite being neither under suspicion of a crime or clinically depressed. I've just been overtaken by events, left lying in the dust. But I don't want to fail in my role as a mother. For Tom, I have to be strong, upright, to fight.

I want his parents to be a source of pride to him.

Wednesday, 18th November 2020

I've been on sick leave for the past two weeks, but inactivity is becoming a problem. Fortunately, writing helps. I feel a sense of liberation at putting words onto paper. I've got a notebook, and use it to keep track of my emotions. It provides distance, helping to keep me from drowning. For me, writing is a form of therapy, a means of rising above the trauma.

But it's time to head back to the office. If nothing else, it should stop me fixating on my father all the time. In any case, I can't hope to have all the answers to my questions before the investigation is finished. I've been informed of the offences with which he's been formally charged: aggravated rape; rape in association with others; administering dangerous substances; invasion of privacy by taking and distributing sexual images. The police have now identified more than 60 of my mother's aggressors and are planning to arrest them in one fell swoop, early in the morning at their homes.

So why continue to obsess about it all? It will all eventually come to a trial, but not before 2024 at the earliest. By then, I'll be ready to face my father, and all the others who took part in the abuse of Mum. She, too, will be steadier on her feet by then.

Assuming that such a thing is possible when you're 68 years old. I miss her terribly.

Monday, 23rd November 2020

Walking into my office building fills me with happiness. I feel reborn! I keep my private problems to myself and just enjoy picking up where I'd left off with the rest of my team. I feel at ease, back where I ought to be. It's a heady feeling.

There's a surprise from my management: they offer me the possibility to change positions and take on a whole new challenge. I'm delighted by the prospect of something new, and relieved to find that I'm so delighted, that I'm capable of bouncing back after all I've been through. And then I remember – this is something I have in common with my father. How many times had I seen him throw himself into a new project after the failure of the previous one?

Tuesday, 24th November 2020

I leave the office feeling proud of myself. It's been a good day, full of new ideas and new projects. I'm back in my stride and Pierre will be delighted to see me this way.

I get into my car and call Mum. I want her to feel upbeat with me. Then she says something that makes me recoil, as if I've been stabbed.

'Your father's in a bad way in prison. He's suffering so much; I must have failed him in some way over the past years.'

I can only hope there's something wrong with my hearing. But no. I try to write it off as a case of Stockholm syndrome, of unwitting sympathy with your torturer, but I can't hide my irritation. Mum puts an end to the call.

When I get home, I can feel something is wrong. I bring

it up with Pierre and he tells me that my brother David has been in touch. My father has written a letter to Sylvie and her husband – friends of Mum's – from his cell in the Pontet jail. Forbidden all communication with the outside, my father passed the letter on to a fellow prisoner, who then sent it out. In other words, my father had managed to game the system designed to prevent him from contacting his victim. The letter reached Mum that morning, having followed her all the way to my brother Florian's house. Opening it was like opening a letter bomb. David sums up its contents: 'He complains that he's been abandoned and demands our help, specifically on the financial front.'

I'm furious. It was culpably naive of my mother's friends to send on the letter. Clearly, they've not understood the nature of the man we're dealing with here. Why had my mother said nothing about it when we were on the phone? Who is she trying to protect? I can draw up a worrying list: my mother knows about the photos of me, but she has shied away from the subject; she stayed away from the psychiatric hospital when I was interned; and now she hides the existence of this letter from me. Has she decided to take the side of her twisted husband? Is my father now stealing my mother from me?

I'm angry because I can see things clearly: this letter isn't a cry for help, it's simply yet another attempt to manipulate his entire family. Even locked up, he's trying to reassert his control over us. And, despite everything, it's close to working, because he can still pluck at Mum and Florian's heartstrings. It's just as well David and I no longer have any illusions about him.

I call my mother, my blood boiling. She puts me on loudspeaker so that Florian can take part in the call.

'Caroline, we'd agreed to keep this from you until we met with the lawyer, but it seems David has let the cat out of the bag.'

'You all agreed? What are you talking about? What exactly do you think you're going to do about this letter?'

'I'm not going to do anything,' she snaps. 'It wasn't addressed to me. He sent it to Sylvie.'

I can tell that Mum is on the verge of tears. Yet another thing to hold against my father. He's behind this, still pulling her strings, making her do whatever he wants.

All it took was one letter. I tell Mum to open her eyes, to wake up to the hold he still has over her. She parries by insisting that she's old enough to think for herself, thank you very much. I try to stay calm, but in the end I start yelling.

I tell her to send me the letter. She refuses point blank.

Without warning, I end the call. I'd imagined I'd mostly pieced myself back together, but now I'm a field of ruins again. I'm angry at Florian for not giving Mum better advice, given she's living with him. I want the letter so that I can send it to our lawyer, but neither will give it to me.

So I go around them. I call Sylvie and explain to her how important it is that this letter be included in the case materials. It's an attempt to manipulate us and, as such, should be shown to the investigating magistrate. Even if its contents were innocuous it was still an illegal document as it broke the rules of the prison. I convince her that it's a serious matter. She sends me, by email, a copy she'd made of the letter. It has all the hallmarks of my father's Machiavellian personality, and I read it in a paroxysm of fury, as if discovering them for the first time.

In it he poses as the victim, humbly asking for mercy and – of course – a little help with his finances. It plainly shows that there are no depths to which he won't plumb.

> Dear friends, I know I've disappointed you, but you're my only possible link to the outside world because I'm not allowed to contact my family, despite the fact that I miss them terribly. I find myself in an awful place, alone, frightened, preoccupied, completely isolated. I know I'm paying the price for what I did to the love of my life, and to my family and friends, but it's too late for that. I've no idea what'll come next, and how this will all end. I'm asking you, in the name of our long

friendship, to gather up some of my things and drop them off at the prison: [my light brown jacket, my grey Adidas top, my Nike shoes, my heavy grey wool sweater, a belt with a small buckle (my two pairs of trousers are too big for me) …]. You can hand in the clothes at the prison entrance, but don't add anything else beyond what I've asked for, assuming you still have the tiniest scrap of friendly feeling towards me …

All I ask is a little pity, a little sympathy. I'll be in prison for a long time. I don't what's going to happen to the house, or everything else for that matter. The hardest thing to face here is the boredom. We only get one hour of exercise per day and we're shut up two to a cell. It's hard on me. I know how deeply I've hurt the woman I love most of all, and that I'll never get over the fact that I'm going to lose my family, my little ones, just as if I'd abandoned them. I can't sleep at night for thinking about it, and I'm losing weight, but I deserve nothing less. I miss all of you and am ashamed of myself. If you're in touch with them – especially my love, who is my entire life – tell them I ask for their forgiveness. Can you send me the dates of my grandchildren's birthdays so that I don't lose track? It's so hard to think that I'll never see my next grandson, Florian's son, who'll be born early next year.

> It'll be a desolate New Year for me. My one hope is that my love manages to get over everything. In here I realise more than ever how much I love her, even if she's demanded a divorce. She'll always be my one true love, the saint I was unable to keep for myself. If you can, send me a letter with the addresses of Caroline, David and Florian, as I've forgotten them. You can't imagine what it's like to be cut off from the rest of the world like this. Send me their phone numbers too, for later on.

What a performance! David shares my scepticism, but that doesn't stop the letter undermining the unity of the family. It reveals my father's cunning – at a time when the four of us ought to stand as one, he manages to create division. The letter is a faithful reflection of its author: pitiful and pathetic. It's so self-centred, all about his suffering and his needs. His indifference to what we're going through is patent. Phrase after phrase ring hollow: 'If you talk to her, tell her I love her.'

The melodrama, the pathos – all his old tricks – none of it comes as a surprise.

I send the letter to our lawyer, so that she can pass it on to the investigating magistrate.

Friday, 27th November 2020

Three days have gone by since I've spoken to Mum. Same for Florian. From behind his bars, my father has managed to split us into two camps.

The first elements of the case files available to civil parties are now in the hands of our lawyer, Caty, including all the interviews with my father since his arrest on the 2nd November, adding up to several hundred pages and filling three binders.

I go to the lawyer's office in person, while Mum prefers to stay at home and deal with it at a distance. In a sad twist of the date: today is my father's 68th birthday. I anticipate a difficult meeting, and gird myself mentally.

Pierre is by my side as I walk into the lawyer's offices, striding across a solemn parquet floor. Caty's team is almost entirely female, which reassures me and boosts my confidence. I've come to see men as a source of danger, ready to grind up pills and abuse their victims for years on end. I now feel uneasy and uncomfortable in the company of men.

Caty is already on the phone with my mum. She had started reading to her, but is happier to have me there too, saying it's better for us both to be present.

For 45 minutes straight, she takes us through some interview transcripts. Time and again, she underlines my father's dishonesty.

When a police officer asks: 'Do you remember going to X's house in Y to sexually abuse his partner?'

My father answers: 'I can't be sure where we were, you know… We agreed to meet on a dirt path after nightfall. He blindfolded me before he led me to his house…'

'Did you sexually abuse his partner that evening?'

'You know, now that you've got me thinking about it, it's coming back to me. That evening I didn't go into their house. I didn't get any further than the garden. The thing was, the pills hadn't done their job.'

My father only admits tiny slivers of truth and, even then, only when he senses that his back is against the wall. That's not all – he reveals a side to his personality I'd never encountered. His vocabulary is crude, humiliating, demeaning when he talks about my mother. The aggressors who took part in the abuse speak in the same vulgar, offensive way. The dialogue in the videos, the messages exchanged through online sites, and the texts on his phone all share the same dirty and degrading quality. After a while, it becomes too much for my mother.

'I'm sorry to interrupt, but I don't think Caroline should be listening to all of this. All of these records are about me. It's all very intimate, and there's no need for Caroline to hear every last detail.'

Delicately, Caty explains to her that, as a civil party to the criminal investigation, I have the legal right to access every single element of the case, whether or not my mother agrees to it. She can ask me to get my own lawyer if she wants to avoid us all being around the same table, but that wouldn't block my access to the information. I know my mother wants to protect me, but I want to know everything there is to know about my father the rapist. Who is this man who proclaimed a boundless admiration for his wife and yet talked about her in such degrading terms?

Under the shade of the mulberry tree, you turn towards me, a glass of pastis in your hand, your eyes sparkling. It's the start of the summer holidays. You ask me about my projects, about what's new at work. Then you go off to clean up the pool, putting on some music and whirling your grandchildren around in a merry dance.

Caty ploughs through the rest of the dossier, a collection of all the different types of records a criminal case can produce: home searches, confiscations, interrogations, etc. They all have one thing in common: the details are sordid.

She reads us the messages that my father posted to the online forums he used to organise the gatherings where my mother was raped.

He was proud of the strength of the cocktail of anxiety medicine he used. He lists his recipe with the aplomb of a mixologist, giving precise doses, counting off the number of Temesta pills to be diluted in alcohol or hidden in food. He warns that the effects may vary if the woman is a smoker, and recommends using alcohol as a solvent, because it gives the best results. Reluctantly, I think again of the photos he took of me. I'm an occasional smoker, especially when taking an aperitif, whereas my mother has never smoked. It sounds to me like he's reporting back on the use of his drug cocktails on me.

He boasts of his ability to plunge my mother into a coma-like state for hours on end: 'Last time, I wasn't generous enough with the doses, but now I'm sure I've got it right. This time we'll really be able to get down to it.'

The messages show that my mother wasn't his only victim. He went to other addresses and abused the partners of men like himself, or at least went with the intention of doing so.

He sought out couples that practised threesomes so that he could join in. On one occasion, he accepted an invitation from a couple to join them in a nudist camp for group sex.

There's an account of a 'failed mission' – his term for an attempted rape. He talks about breaking into the room of a woman he'd never met, in the middle of the night. Presumably, this woman suspected that her partner had been up to no good, and hadn't touched the drink he had served her beforehand. When my father approached her bed she turned on the light. 'Caught like a rabbit in the headlights', my father fled the scene. In retelling the story, he tries to give it a comic spin: 'I felt so bloody stupid. Just as I take down my trousers, on come the lights and up she jumps!' He goes on to reproach his host with careless preparation and with having sabotaged his 'mission'. Worried about being caught – which of course indicates that he was fully aware of the gravity of his acts – my father asked the woman's partner to delete all trace of their exchanges.

I can't contain myself. Exactly how many women has my father raped? I feel I'm peering down a bottomless well.

> We're on a small motorboat off the Corsican coast in a very rough sea. You tell me to stay calm and reassure me we'll be alright. I stop being afraid and we work together to steer the boat to safety.

The lawyer draws our attention to an exchange with a man who is proposing to offer up his wife for rape. Talking about what to do if any children happen to be present in the house at the time, my father says: 'just give them a jab with their dinner.' Caty notices me seizing up and hurriedly adds that it's not clear whether the assault actually happened in this particular case.

My father shares his morbid fantasies with the men he talks to and tries to work out just how motivated they are to follow his lead. His starting point is always the same – a hookup site called *Coco*. He reaches out to men and asks them if, like him, they like 'rape-style sex' and quizzes them on the sex acts they're interested in. This is the preliminary stage of his process, before inviting them to the house.

To attract potential abusers and draw them into action, he posts photos of my mother – unconscious and provocatively posed, in the vast majority of cases – in a private forum called 'Behind her back'. He dresses my mother like a cheap prostitute. As bait, it works all too well.

Almost all my mother's aggressors live in Provence, the majority within a short driving distance. He hand-draws and photographs little maps to guide them right to the door of the house. Sometimes he sends them final instructions by text as they reach their destination.

So as not to alert the neighbours, they're all told to park

outside a nearby sports facility. Although most of the time there's only one aggressor, sometimes he invites several of them at once. They're told not to smoke or wear aftershave. They must leave their phones in their cars, to avoid the risk of an unexpected call waking my mother up.

He makes them get undressed in the kitchen and leave their clothes outside the front door, just in case they have to leave in a hurry. They have to wash their hands in hot water, in case a cold touch wakes my mother, even momentarily. He offers to show them videos of previous rapes, to get them excited and make sure they know what to expect. He reminds them that they must avoid making any noise – nothing louder than a whisper – once they enter the overheated bedroom.

The videos show that my mother's unconscious state provokes no hesitation amongst the aggressors. If anything, it seems to embolden them. Inevitably, the police quiz him on how well the men he brought in were informed about my mother's drugged state. His answer is that he systematically explained to them that he had administered a chemical cocktail that would ensure she remained unconscious.

Questions about his sexual interest in his own daughter are met by a categorical denial. He evades the subject completely. When confronted with the photos of me semi-clothed and unconscious, he denies ever having seen them before.

He insists they have nothing to do with him. He has no problem identifying me, however: 'Yes, that's certainly my daughter, but beyond that I can tell you nothing about these photos. Look how young she is – much younger than the women I take an interest in. There's nothing sexual about these. Look at all the other images you've found on my devices – they're very different from these.' Summing up his position, he declares: 'I've never laid a finger on my daughter.'

Listening to the interviews with my father leaves me in a smouldering rage. My mother, on the other end of a phone in my brother's house, doesn't appear to have grasped the devastating nature of what is, after all, his own account of his deeds. Let's not forget that we're talking about a man who prided himself on being a good husband and father.

Caty has spent hours reading to us, and afternoon has shaded into evening. Even so, I'm convinced we still have more to discover about my father. I'm forced to admit that my mother and I will probably never come to the same conclusions about the man and all that he has done. I sense that she'll seek refuge in some form of denial – a protection mechanism for her, but one that I won't be able to tolerate if she tries it in my company.

It's time to stop for the day. I'm exhausted and a migraine is taking hold of my skull.

Thursday, 10th December 2020

The psychiatric expert appointed by the investigating magistrate has summoned me. The objective of the meeting is to determine the impact of the news of my father's crimes on my mental wellbeing.

It's almost 7pm when I reach the address I've been given – a glass and concrete building dating from the 80s – and enter what looks more like an apartment than a doctor's office.

I feel uneasy, wary of telling my tale to a stranger, and a man to boot. This anxiety has been with me since the day I received the summons, some weeks before. It's an indication of how fragile I remain.

African masks and photos of foreign lands decorate the waiting room. A well-groomed man with grey hair wearing a dark suit appears and invites me into his cramped consultation room.

I instinctively scan the four corners of the tiny space, but there's no way out. A bookshelf heaped with books on psychiatry and the behavioural sciences towers over me.

He studies me silently for a long time. I don't move a muscle.

'Let me explain to you how this interview will play out. First of all, I want you to tell me about your childhood, your adolescence, your adult life as it was *before*, and as it is now. I want to hear about the role your father played within the family. We'll close with some multiple-choice questionnaires to allow me to evaluate the nature and the depth of your trauma. And, of course, the extent to which it impinges upon your day-to-day life.'

I don't hesitate. The words pour out of me.

'I'm the second of three children, with an elder and a younger brother.

'I have a bachelor's degree from university. I've always worked hard to get what I wanted – probably because money was often tight when I was growing up. My parents didn't shield me from their marital disputes or frequent money problems. I learned early on what 'this is a serious problem' means. I'd witnessed a scene of domestic violence by the time I was nine. My father grabbed the collar of my mother's blouse, hauling her off her feet and slamming her against the bathroom wall. I was sure then she wanted to leave him. Later on, after another act of violence, that's exactly what she did.

'One day, when I was 14, I came home from school for lunch and found a bailiff, a police officer, and a bunch of moving men loading up all the furniture from our lounge to take it away. My father knew they were coming and had hidden away the things he deemed essential, like the TV and the stereo equipment. He poured abuse on the movers as they left in their van. I put the blame squarely on him, angry that my mother would come home later that day to an almost empty house. I still recall my father walking up and down the lounge, his face livid, crying like a little boy. I wanted to cry, too. They'd taken away a chest of drawers that my grandfather had passed on to my mother when he died. Built of marble and polished wood, it had always taken pride of place in the lounge. It was my only remaining connection with my maternal grandfather. I had been very close to him. He'd made the most of himself, joining the army and spending his entire career in uniform. Despite all he'd had to overcome and his fragile health, he remained to the end a man of principle, determined, ambitious and – more than anything – generous. The one keepsake I had of him had been carted off, to be sold at auction like a worthless trinket.

'That year, we celebrated Christmas sitting indoors on garden furniture. But that didn't stop my father unveiling a golden ring with semiprecious stones as a present for my mother. He was trying to make it up to her, like a guilty adolescent. She immediately told him to return it to the jewellers and get the money back.'

It's like a dam has burst. I can't stop the words pouring out of me.

'A few years later, I discovered that my father had been secretly taking money from the kitty I'd saved up while working summer jobs. He was shameless when I confronted him, telling me that he was within his rights, and that he'd pay me back soon enough. When I looked at the other families around us, I realised that ours was somehow upside down, that it wasn't normal I had to play the parent to my father. I felt responsible for him, saw him as someone who didn't think things through and couldn't be counted upon. I felt bound to help him, even though I was a child.

'I often got pulled into arguments and discussions between my father and mother that I should never have witnessed. They would rope me in, both trying to get me onto their side. I learned to hide away at my friends' houses. Only there could I turn my back on all these grown-up problems.

'My father was always trying to game the system and prove that he could finally overcome his problems. A trained electrician, every time he tried his hand at something different he couldn't pull it off. Failure was always waiting for him, especially when he decided to set up his own company. The funding came from my brothers and myself. We lent him the capital for his firm, but it didn't last long. When it went bust, he was even deeper in the red than before.

'His misplaced ambition and poor decision-making skills created problems for all of us. Luckily, my mother had a steady middle-management job, working for the same company for over 20 years. Thanks to her employers, for 16 years, starting in the 1990s, we lived in a company-provided house with five bedrooms and a walled garden in a coveted neighbourhood on the banks of the river Marne just outside Paris.

'Despite all his failings, my father was always there for his kids, ready to listen to and encourage us. When I wanted to give up on my modern dance classes, he heard me out and patiently explained why I should keep going – which I did, remaining a committed dancer until my mid-twenties. When I was thirteen he sought out my dance teacher, insisting that they have a serious conversation about whether I should consider a professional career in dance.

'So, I suppose there means there was a point in time when my father had a normal life. He would get up early in the morning to drive me to school so that I wouldn't have to take the bus. Before I got my driving licence, he was always willing to ferry me about at weekends, picking me up in the middle of the night if necessary. He would comfort me when I had boyfriend problems, or when my mother and I were caught up in one of our disputes.

'He set the same objective for all three of his children: we should do better than he had. This was a constant theme during our teenage years.

'He regretted the fact that he had missed out on a proper education. He often spoke to us about his early years, about his difficult childhood and how his father took him out of school and made him start working at age 13. His parents were caretakers at a rehabilitation centre for convicts called Château d'Oublaise in the centre of France. Having learned on the job, he ultimately became a qualified electrician, working on building sites scattered across the country and then in the Paris region. His earnings contributed to his parents' upkeep. In his rendition his father was a marginal figure, too lazy to work, happy to live on the backs of others, despite the fact that he had many practical skills. My father turned out much the same, with a similar taste for improvised and unstable solutions.

'As we grew older, my brothers and I learned to live with my father's ever-shifting personality. He couldn't hide his frustration and his jealous nature. When reality didn't suit him, he would try disguise it, make things out to be better than they were. We were rarely fooled. But we loved him all the same and learned to live with his faults.'

The psychiatrist says it's time for a pause.

We sit in silence for a while, then he asks me to lay my hand flat out on his desk. Then he tells me to lift it up. He's trying to evaluate my level of stress – am I calmly telling my tale, or is it flooding me with emotions? I do what he asks, leaving the sweaty outline of my fingers on the desktop. He looks at me, the very picture of professional detachment.

'How do you feel?'

'Betrayed. And ashamed to be the daughter of such a torturer.'

Saturday, 12th December 2020

I've not heard from Florian since the 24th November, the day we clashed over my father's letter. He and my mother have decided to handle her final move from the house in Provence on their own. They're going to take a train down, rent a truck, recover what remains of her past, and bring it back to Florian's house in the Parisian suburbs.

All my mother has to show for the last ten years of her life are a few carboard boxes, some clothes and some bedding. Everything else has been tossed, sold or given away.

My mother wants my father to have a few more things in prison. She's made up a bag with warm clothes and some personal items, to be dropped off at the prison in Le Pontet. My father's closest friends all refused to help him out once they learned why he'd been imprisoned.

When she gets there, the prison guard explains that they can't accept any deliveries on weekends. My father won't get the package until the middle of the following week, once its contents have been sorted and verified.

I learn all this with disbelief. My mother is fussing over the man who allowed her to be raped for ten years running.

Monday, 14th December 2020

My alarm goes off at 5:30am. I have to catch a train to Avignon, where I'm to meet with the investigating magistrate. I'm in my brother David's house, having spent the previous evening with him, his wife and their children. David insists on dropping me off at the station. He gets up at the same time as me. Céline, my sister-in-law, comes to hug me just before me leave.

Deep down inside, I'm afraid I might lose heart and give up the struggle. When I'm with the judge there'll be no one by my side. Everything I say could have an impact on the way the case plays out. It's a huge responsibility.

Arriving in Avignon unleashes a wave of memories of my father from my life *before*: me peering at the noticeboard where results of the baccalaureate have been pinned up and turning to him to receive his congratulations; me going up to receive my degree, a few years further down the line, and looking out at him as he beams with pride; me introducing him to Pierre, the man destined to be my husband, and knowing he's delighted that I've finally found someone right for me; him and me in the Olympia concert hall in 2011, both of us carried away by the music; him singing a long and tender song written by Jean-Louis Aubert on my wedding day in 2009, infusing it with feeling.

These were once happy memories, but now their resurgence makes me feel like I'm being waterboarded by the past.

The judge's office is on the fourth floor. I'm an hour early. I take a seat in an ugly, jaundiced corridor. I feel like I've been cast in a low-budget police procedural.

My mother's in there right now, being questioned by the judge. Her appointment was for 10am, an hour before mine. At midday, I'm still waiting. Caty, who is there to accompany both of us, pops out to tell me that my mother's interview has run over. All told, it lasts for three and a half hours. During this time, I walk aimlessly up and down the corridors of the courthouse. A dusty silence muffles my footsteps.

When my mother finally emerges, she is exhausted. At 1:30pm, I take her place alongside Caty in a spacious room with windows half-open to the street outside. The judge is a young woman. The innumerable files piled up on her desk hide all but her face and her straight-cut, light-chestnut hair. The court reporter sits to her right, poised over her laptop.

The judge informs me that she has asked to see me in the context of the complaint I filed against my father on the 3rd November 2020. That small formality over, I begin to talk.

'I'm absolutely convinced that my father's deviant behaviour didn't start in 2013. I can't say precisely when it did, but I recall my brother Florian telling me a disturbing story in 2011. At that time, Florian and his girlfriend – now his wife – were living with my parents. One day, his girlfriend walked in on my father masturbating behind his computer in his office. He'd left the door wide open. In her embarrassment, she turned on her heels and sought refuge in the bedroom she shared with Florian.

'A few months later, I told my mother this story. She had been puzzled by the fact that Florian had been absent from several family get-togethers. My father had noticed it too, and had started openly complaining about it. When my mother passed my explanation for this on to my father, he reacted with violent indignation.'

The judge signals me to pause. She asks the court reporter if she caught everything. Then she asks me about my mother's repeated episodes of memory loss.

'I'm pretty sure that my father drugged her even when they were staying in my house. In December 2019, my husband and I took our son to Morocco during the Christmas holidays and we invited my parents to stay in our place while we were away. Later, my mother told me how she'd lost consciousness on the evening of the 28th December when they'd invited over a couple of friends. She remembers getting ready for their arrival, but nothing after that – not greeting them as they arrived or watching them leave. And yet she wasn't at all tired, since she was retired by then, she hadn't spent time with her grandchildren for over a month and was having a quiet Christmas with my father.

'I just figured she was ill. Shortly after they arrived in Paris mid-December, she'd told me she was bleeding heavily. Given that her menopause was long behind her, I was seriously concerned and made an urgent appointment for her with my gynaecologist. The doctor detected an inflammation of her uterine passage and prescribed some antifungal ointment for a few days, and we didn't pursue it any further.

'Throughout those years, my mother had many absent moments. Knowing what we do now, I'm sure my father drugged her in May 2019 when she and my father were staying in a holiday home Pierre and I have.'

'Why do you say that?' asked the judge.

'My mother had no memory of having tidied up the house, or emptying the bins, or locking the door on the morning they left. I know they set off that day before ten in the morning, and I think she must have lost consciousness almost as soon as they started driving. Which says a lot about the strength of the doses my father inflicted upon her, even in the morning, dissolved in her coffee. Not once does he seem to have thought that, with her slight frame, her body might not be able to cope.

'I tried to call her several times that morning, but never got through. Finally, my father answered her mobile phone and said that they were passing the outskirts of Lyon and that she was fast asleep. I recall his exact words: "Your mother's exhausted. She was so concerned about leaving the house as clean and tidy as possible that she ran herself ragged, as she always does. But she finally managed to calm down and doze off."

'Having shared many long trips with my mother, I'd never seen her fall asleep in a car, so I found the whole thing rather worrying.

'Now I know – it's there in the evidence the enquiry has gathered – that he'd drugged her so as to serve her up to men on the motorway service areas on their way back to Provence. I didn't manage to speak to her until late the next day. The last thing she could remember was standing outside our holiday home with her hands on the key in the lock. Of the rest of the day and the long trip home: nothing. She didn't wake up until my father turned into the driveway of their house in Mazan. She had slept eight hours straight.'

I stop myself and look up at the judge.

I'm aware how my recollections can help to flesh out my father's otherwise impenetrable personality. From a legal point of view, I have to be ready to stand behind everything I say, to insist on the truth even if it means accepting the destruction of my family. Whatever price I have to pay, I can't step back. Not faced with so many crimes, so many rapes, so many guilty men. The case, involving my father and all the other accused men, is massive, and I feel very small and very alone in its shadow. I feel guilty too. I can't hide behind the fact that I saw nothing at the time, because I ought to have seen something, I ought to have been more discerning, I ought to have tried harder to unearth the cause of my mother's episodes of memory loss. I was too trusting and I can't forgive myself for it.

I'm not finished with the judge. I have other concerns, ones that go beyond establishing my father's actions. I want her to understand how much we, his children, now suffer because of the way he manipulated us. Could we have known that he was such a constant liar, that playing a role came so naturally to him? Could we have pierced through the mask he wore in the normal, everyday world? Should the weeks he spent in our homes, in our company, have been enough to allows us to see the truth?

I decide to tell the judge about a day in August 2019 that had stayed with me.

I'd just had the last of three operations in an attempt to put an end to five months of vaginal pain from a tear that refused to heal. None of the surgeons who had worked on me could explain the origin of the problem. Throughout those months I felt diminished, crippled by pain but unable to talk about it. Now, a new question torments me: were the two photos taken of me, and whatever else my father did, behind all that suffering?

That summer I'd been rushed to the hospital for an urgent operation after an initial intervention had caused complications. Then, three weeks later, the same thing happened, this time while I was away on holiday. On Saturday the 10th August, I was supposedly recovering in bed, but the pain was still intense and the previous night had been without sleep. At 10:45am, my phone buzzes. I pick it up off the bedside table and discover that I've missed four calls from my father. He's also left a text message: 'Call me ASAP. It's urgent.'

Ever naive, I assume he wants to know about my operation and recovery, but when I call him back I'm greeted with a brusque, businesslike tone: 'Sorry. I know it's not a good time, but I need your help.'

The same old story ensues. He says he needs a hundred euros there and then to ensure that his bank account doesn't go into the red. He doesn't have an overdraft and says that the recent visit of his three grandchildren that July – including Tom – has pushed him financially over the edge. Once again, I tell myself that I'll never get to be the child in this family, never be freed of the obligation to help my father solve his problems. I'm getting tired of this constant role reversal: 'I don't want your mother to know. She's already over-anxious as it is. So don't tell her anything, I'll handle everything…'

It's not an accident that I'm the one he's called, rather than David or Florian. He knows I'll help him out without asking any questions. It's become a habit. I've never been able to tell him no, to make him take responsibility for the situation he finds himself in. This he knows all too well.

That's how manipulation works. We know our strings are being pulled, but we can't escape it, we simply accept that's how things are. I'm too tired to argue and tell him that I'll transfer the money. I try to sound indifferent, but inside I'm angry with both of us.

Ten minutes later he calls me back.

'Caro, it won't be enough. I need another twenty. If you can transfer a hundred and twenty right now …'

The cheek of the man leaves me speechless. I'm recovering from an operation and he calls me with a dodgy story and a demand for money? Of course, I shouldn't be surprised. It's not like it's the first it's happened, but this is bordering on the indecent.

The phone rings again. The third call in less than twenty minutes.

'Caro, now that I think of it, a hundred a forty would be better. That'll tide me over until my pension comes through.'

'I'm not your bank.'

'It's just a favour. Surely you can do me a favour? If not for me, for your mother. You don't have to worry; you'll get the money back.'

I hang up, my heart beating and my fists clutched in frustration. He's playing the guilt card. And it's working. The next day I sent him a text to say he doesn't have to pay me back. Needless to say, he makes no attempt to contradict me.

I avoid talking to my parents until the end of the month, when we all get together for David's birthday. My father is distant with me, telling me that my behaviour had been 'unacceptable'. The cherry on the cake. I wait a few days and then call my mother to tell her everything. I'm fed up running after them like they were little kids.

The judge hears me out attentively. Then she asks if I have anything else to add.

'I do. My niece Sasha – she's nine years old, one of my brother David's girls – told me something astonishing after my father was imprisoned. She remembered, back during the winter holidays of February 2019, seeing her grandmother asleep on her back with her arms thrown out. She said she was sleeping so soundly that nothing my niece said could wake her up. Eventually her grandfather told her to leave her gran in peace. According to Sasha, her gran hadn't woken up that day until almost lunchtime. My mother never sleeps that late, and certainly not when she has her grandchildren staying with her.'

I'm presented with the record of my statements. I read it through and sign it. Soon my father will be confronted with this document. I feel like I've finally taken the gloves off. For the first time, I'm convinced it's what he deserves. I'm going to tear the veil off all these years of lies and manipulations.

When I leave the judge's office, Mum has nothing to say. I realise that, psychologically speaking, she can't face the truth, accept that the unthinkable has happened. It's too much for her. She wants to convince herself that the man she loved so long wasn't so sexually depraved from the outset. She wants to find some kind of an excuse for him, some kind of attenuating circumstances.

Back at the station, we each take a different train back to Paris, a symbol of the different trajectories we've chosen.

I slump down in my allocated seat, utterly exhausted. I feel grimy. I'm ashamed to have loved the father I thought I knew.

Thursday, 17th December 2020

Mum and I are becoming distant. It's inconceivable for her that I too might have been one of my father's victims. Inconceivable because it's too painful to contemplate, which I completely understand. I do nonetheless resent the fact that she won't even consider the possibility, and take the time to listen to my anger and pain. Mum just keeps telling me to stop putting myself through such nervous and mental stress. Officially, nothing indicates that I was a victim of chemical submission. Nothing proves I'd been touched in any way, let alone raped. But I find no peace of mind in the absence of proof.

I know that my mother has been through worse than me and is doing her best to deal with it. She's in survival mode, shutting down so as to protect herself from the intolerable.

But I have gone to war, intent on crossing swords with my own demons.

Still working from home, I use the time between meetings to maintain the house in an impeccable state. I clean, discard, and organise, but what I'm really trying to do is tidy away the question that obsesses me: Did my father abuse me?

> You pick Tom up and carry him into the pool. The sun flashes off the surface of the turquoise water. You tell him that today he's going to swim without his armbands. Quietly, confidentially, you assure him that everything will be fine, that you'll be right beside him. You stand in the middle of the pool, holding him against you. Tom isn't afraid. He releases his arms from around your neck. He's ready to give it a go, trusting that you're right and that he can do it. I watch from the side of the pool. I'm not afraid either. I, too, trust you.

I open a cupboard full of bedding. A folded-up sheet catches my attention. I recognise the pattern. I bought it just before Tom was born. A second later I've collapsed and am down on my knees on the floor.

The sheet features in one of the photos that I was shown

in the police station in Carpentras in November. It's the same pattern. My father photographed me in my house, in my bedroom, way back in 2013. There's no room for doubt anymore. His second victim was me.

Thursday, 24th December 2020

For the first time in his life, Tom will not spend Christmas surrounded by his grandparents and all his cousins. Our family has been torn in two: I will be at David's place; Mum will be at Florian's. From now on, traditional family get-togethers will be, at best, half-baked. My father's hard at work with the age-old tactic of divide and conquer. He has destroyed what meant the most to us: our existence as a family unit, our shared roots.

I announce a symbolic decision: to free him from this curse, I'm going to change one of my son's middle names – Dominique – which, as a loving daughter, was given as a nod to my father. My eldest brother's name – David – will take its place. As soon as I can, I'll contact the registry office and start the process.

David, not the most effusive of men, can't find the words but pulls me into a hug.

Friday, 1st January 2021

The first day of a new year, and I'm thinking about my father. For the first time ever, I feel compassion for him. I imagine what it must be like in his cell. Is he cold? Hungry? Who are his cellmates? How is he coping with being deprived of his beloved bike rides?

I realise I still have progress to make. I've not yet reached the point where I can treat such questions with utter indifference. The point where my father means nothing to me.

I've heard nothing from Mum since Christmas. I miss her. I decide to give her a call. When I hear her voice I start crying. She soon follows suit. Tears have become our default language, because what we're going through is beyond words.

Eventually, I manage to express myself: I want to be with her, to stand by her. We talk for the next two hours. At the end, we promise each other we'll stick together from now on. And that neither will sit in judgement of the other.

Saturday, 23rd January 2021

I'm in a good mood when I wake up. It's a cold, clear, invigorating day. I set off to the market under a cloudless sky. Tonight, we're invited to David's house to celebrate two birthdays – mine and his wife, Céline's, who has done so much for me over the past months.

It's the first weekend since the 2nd November that I actually enjoy. The day is spent idly but agreeably and at around 5pm we get in the car to head off to my brother's.

It proves too good to be true. We're still en route when Mum calls me. She's back down in Provence, tying up some administrative loose ends.

'Caro, have you been in contact with the family members of one of the prisoners in Le Pontet jail?'

'Mum, are you crazy? What on earth could make you think that?'

I can tell something has unsettled her. She tells me that she's received a second letter from my father. In it, he says his life is in danger. And that it's my fault.

Nothing my twisted father might say could surprise me. But it's a gut punch to think that my mother might believe him. We're back to where we were: he's pulling her strings, manoeuvring to further his game plan. I tell Mum to send me the letter. I want to see what he's invented this time round.

The letter, dated the 9th January, was delivered to Sylvie, my mother's friend. Just like the last time. Once again, my father has succeeded in finding a way around the prison system. By the time we reach David's house, I can't hold back my sobs.

I hate my manipulating father, and I can't help being annoyed at the way my mother lets him play her. I'd like to salvage the evening, but it's difficult. Shut up in his cell, my father has ruined my party.

Sunday, 24th January 2021

Next morning, I read the letter in utter disbelief.

> I imagine it was you, my dear brother Michel, who dropped off those warm clothes smelling of home. On them I found a hair that came from the love of my life, and it warmed my heart for a few seconds.
>
> I share a cell with a young prisoner whose parents tried to find out more about me by telephone, since they didn't know what I'm in for, but Caroline told them everything, so my cellmate doesn't want to be near me anymore. Try to calm her down because she'll end up getting me lynched. There's no forgiveness here, so it's urgent. I'm going to be forced to spend the rest of my life in prison, or at

> least as long as I can keep on going without any news from outside. It's too hard, and anyway everyone'll be happy to see me go. I'm not asking for pity, just a little warmth. Life here is too hard, and Caroline's anger makes it worse.

My father's perversity knows no bounds. He has all the time in the world to find ways to profit from my mother's naivety and provoke my anger in the hope of dividing us. I know he's a sick man, and he's lost and alone inside his head, but I'd still like to rip it right off.

I need a few days to come to terms with it all.

Sick to the stomach, I don't know whether to give in or rise up and fight.

Thursday, 28th January 2021

I'm working at home, taking part in an online meeting, when Pierre drops an envelope onto my desk. It looks official.

> Having duly examined your request, submitted as his legal representative, to change the first name of Tom Jean Dominique, born the 25th July 2014 in the sixteenth arrondissement of Paris, and having reviewed the supporting documents provided, it has been concluded that the change is motived by legitimate concerns, as defined by article 60 of the Civil Code. In consequence, your son is henceforth authorised to use the first name Tom Jean David.

The relief is immense. Pierre feels it too. If I hadn't gone through with this, I would have felt guilty of neglect. I've done something important to protect my son, who is worth so much more than his forebears.

Buoyed up by the news, I even dash off a short note to my father.

I never send it – my lawyer tells me not to – but it felt good to write.

Dominique,

Three months in prison, four letters stuffed with lies.

You've always known what you're doing, and you keep at it even now.

But there's a difference: I now know who you really are. We all do.

So I'm telling you, stop all your scheming. Right now.

Nothing will stop me pursuing this case. We're all in this to the end.

You're dead to me. Definitively.

Tuesday, 2nd February 2021

We've asked for contributions to help my mother pay for her divorce case. My father isn't contesting it, and the obligatory first appearance before a civil judge is scheduled for the 31st May in Carpentras. My mother will be there in person. My father will be on a video link from prison.

She's hard at work on a debt forgiveness application, hoping to restart life under her maiden name a little less in debt.

Sometimes, when she spends a few days with us at home, I come across her silent and immobile in a corner. She remains a very private person, and doesn't want her distress to be seen. But the wave of contributions coming in has helped to raise her spirits. I've spent weeks reaching out right and left to drum up as much financial support as I can.

I want her to find her confidence and dignity again.

The generosity we've encountered is extraordinary and won't be forgotten. So many people we know have stepped up, proving to my mother that she has not been abandoned in the midst of her troubles. She's more upbeat and has started thinking positively about the future.

She's realised that she's not alone in another sense too. Messages of solidarity have poured in, confirming that rapes don't only happen in underground car parks or in dark alleys behind tower blocks. The vast majority are carried out within the victim's immediate circle. Fathers, brothers, grandfathers, friends and cousins commit rape. Husbands too.

Sunday, 7th February 2021

We've spent the weekend in the countryside, letting the fresh air blow through us.

We've had fun, but I can see something sad in my son's eyes. He's keeping to himself. Out of respect for his feelings, I don't bring it up. But at bedtime, he sits down on his bedspread and tells me that he's made a decision:

'I think a lot about Grandad since he went to prison. Remember you told me I could go and see a nice doctor to talk about it, if I wanted to? Well I do. I really do. I think I need to. I want to get him out of my head. Forever.'

Tuesday, 2nd March 2021

Céline and Aurore – David's and Florian's wives – are called in to their local police stations. At first, we imagine the investigating magistrate is just covering all the bases after my interview with her last December.

Both are kept in for over two hours. Turns out, it's not a simple formality. It's a new episode in my family's horror story.

Naked photos were taken, without their knowledge, of both at different points over the past ten years. My father had installed automatic cameras in bathrooms and bedrooms in their homes and in his. When the family got together, his spy cameras went into action.

He'd used the results to create montages featuring Céline, complete with obscene captions, starting from when she was pregnant in 2011. He collected a set of intimate photos of Aurore from her most recent summer visit to the house in Provence. He took photos of himself masturbating with Aurore's underwear.

He shared them all, posting them online for his fellow sexual deviants.

A new phase in the case opens. Céline and Aurore join me as civil parties to the prosecution, and ask Caty to be their lawyer too.

Not a single woman in my family has been spared by my father.

Over the next few days, 18 men are arrested and taken into custody under suspicion of having raped my mother. My father is moved to a different prison. It's for his own safety. Sexual predators are the lowest of the low inside prisons and fellow detainees sometimes decide to take punishment into their own hands.

Can my father cope with being shuttled from prison to prison? Will he be able to adapt to new surroundings? Of course he will. He's a chameleon. Look how well he pretended to be part of our family for over 40 years.

Wednesday, 10th March 2021

Over the past months, I've witnessed a whole series of women speaking out courageously about the sexual crimes and violence they've suffered. It brings me a form of relief, knowing that what was once unsayable can be voiced so effectively. Two books in particular – Vanessa Springora's *Consent* and Camille Kouchner's *The Familia Grande* – touch me deeply. Both express how they had felt imprisoned by the past, how the crimes of others had tainted their souvenirs and compromised their futures. And yet both had found the strength to denounce what had been done to them, setting it all down on paper.

At least, unlike some other predators, my father won't dare claim that my mother gave her full and free consent to his acts. Not unless he believes that someone in a state of chemical submission remains compos mentis. The tawdry truth is that most of the time rapists bear no resemblance to the dangerous psychopaths of TV series. They look like respectable family men nobody would hesitate to invite over for dinner.

For weeks now, I've wanted to connect with those who fight for women's rights. My mother, whose entire world was pulled out from under her, is a prime example of what's wrong with the system. Next to nothing was done to help her, neither at the moment of crisis nor through its seemingly endless aftermath. Left to fight for herself, she at least had us. How do the women with neither family nor money survive?

An article about a Franco-Lebanese gynaecologist and obstetrician called Ghada Hatem-Gantzer spurs me into action. A leading figure in the fight to end violence against women, she focuses as much on preventing it as dealing with its consequences. I recall having read about her some years previously. I draw from her words the conviction that personal survival isn't enough; I should act to tackle the roots of the problem.

The last few months have shown me conclusively that violence inflicted upon a family requires a systemic response. Every single person linked to a victim is impacted in a significant way. Trauma expands outwards like a shockwave, and the collateral damage cannot be ignored. Immediate psychological care and the ongoing presence of a functional support system is imperative if those who have been scarred are to have a chance to heal.

Today, I have an appointment with Dr Hatem-Gantzer herself at the Women's Centre attached to the main hospital complex in Saint-Denis, a suburb to the north of Paris. She founded this special unit, dedicated to women who have suffered physical or sexual violence, in 2016. Three clinics operate within its walls, dealing with violence, family planning and the victims of sexual mutilation.

Ghada knows nothing about me when she welcomes me to the tiny room that functions as her office. She immediately puts me at ease. Listening to her calm, soothing voice, I open up. I give her a brief account of my own experiences and then talk to her about my growing convictions, hopes and doubts.

Ghada is a pioneer, and has never hesitated to take the first step. Talking to her gives me strength, encourages me to act. Our first meeting marks the birth of a joint project and of a cherished friendship.

That very day, at a press conference with Elisabeth Moreno, the minister for equality, Ghada launches an initiative called Re#start to encourage and coordinate agencies supporting female victims of violence all across the country. If there had been a Women's Centre near me a few months ago, I would have taken my mother there without hesitation. Whether or not female victims obtain competent, professional support and are put in touch with the organisations best equipped to help them shouldn't be a lottery, a question of sheer luck or social standing. The way things are right now, it's the victim who has to take the initiative, and all too often help is inaccessible. We take the walking wounded and abandon them in front of an obstacle course.

Ghada explains to me how hard it is to find the resources she requires, both financial and human. She's trying to scrape enough together to create a safe house in the centre of Paris called 'My Doorstep' to accommodate young women between 18 and 25 who have suffered violence. I tell her I'll help her in any way I can. It will do me good to leave behind my constant tête-à-tête with my own problems, to look beyond them to a broader solution.

Today the Re#start network includes nine fully functioning centres: in Saint-Denis (attached to the Delafontaine hospital complex, opened in July 2016), in Brussels (attached to the Saint-Pierre teaching hospital, opened in September 2017), in Bordeaux (attached to the CACIS sexual health centre, opened in February 2019), in Brive-la-Gaillarde (attached to the Brive hospital complex, opened in November 2020), in Paris (attached to the La-Pitié-Saltpêtrière hospital, opened in January 2021), in Reims (attached to the Le Mars centre for victims of crime, opened in June 2021), in Tours (attached to the Tours teaching hospital, opened in November 2021), in Marseille (attached to the teaching hospital La Conception, opened in January 2022), and in Versailles/Plaisir (attached to the Plaisir hospital complex, opened in January 2022). A dozen more Women's Centres are under development across the country. All work seamlessly with local hospitals to ensure that victims are offered a full spectrum of medical, psychological and social support. At the same time, they liaise with the police and judicial system to ensure no one falls through the net.

Wednesday, 31st March 2021

I introduce Ghada Hatem-Gantzer to my employers, organising a visit for top management to the Women's Centre in Saint-Denis. This gives Ghada an opportunity to pitch them the 'My Doorstep' project. It centres on a 33-bed hotel on boulevard Rochechouart in Paris, which is slated for redevelopment. My employers agree to help her bring the project to completion in as short a time as possible. The goal is to create a refuge for young women, an attractive and comfortable place for them to recover from the violence they have suffered.

The 'My Doorstep' project is a revelation for me, and I'm sure it won't be my last. I've found my cause.

Winter 1990. The Risoul ski station, perched high in the southern Alps. You encourage me to try my first ever red ski run. You say you'll do it with me, since I'm not a great skier and the slopes still have many secrets for me. It's a bright day, but very cold. When we reach the top of the run, you push off without me, shooting off like a rocket. Terrified, I follow. My skies are sticky and I slow down at every bump and curve. It takes me almost two hours to reach the bottom. Through my tears I yell at you for abandoning me. All you say is: 'You made it. Like I said you would.'

Sunday, 5th April 2021

Yesterday evening I talked with my mother, who's currently living with David and Céline. She still refuses to believe that my father could have preyed upon his own daughter. 'Stop tormenting yourself. Your father is incapable of such a thing. I just can't believe it… Because, if I could, it would destroy me utterly.' I realise how different I am from my mother. Her psychological defence mechanisms leave me perplexed.

The call torments me, and I go to bed still tussling with my feelings. At 4:43am, I wake up in a fever, aching all over. I can neither breath nor swallow, still under the sway of my nightmare: My father escapes from prison with my mother's help. The two of them flee to the old house where my brothers and I grew up. I'm there and I confront my father in the garden. He begs me to help him, to hide him somewhere safe. I tell him to go away, but he refuses. My mother pleads on his behalf, but I ignore her and call the police.

I finally get up at 8:30am. My throat has got worse. I can't speak. I call a doctor for a house visit, and he gives me a diagnosis of uvulitis, severe swelling at the back of the throat. He can't find any obvious cause. 'Could be psychosomatic. Do you have any particular anxieties at the moment?'

Friday, 9th April 2021

At 7:19am, Marius joins the family. Florian finally has a son. We don't tell my father. We never will. This particular grandchild will not figure in his recollections.

There's an old saying that a death in a family makes way for a birth. David posts a message to his brother Florian through our WhatsApp group. It is unforgettable.

> Welcome Marius. We lost an old oak we used to lean against but we've gained a young sapling we're all going to keep safe.

Tuesday, 13th April 2021

More men have been arrested, taken from their homes and thrown in jail. Several of them are fathers of young children. I feel for them, these sons and daughters ground underfoot by their fathers, the defacers of their memories, the undertakers of their families. I anticipate what awaits these children as they grow up – the same abyss; the same ruptured, tainted bonds; the same need to cut themselves free, whatever it costs.

Every single bail request is denied.

Friday, 16th April 2021

My lawyer has just received an updated copy of the case file. It contains several hundred pages of interview transcripts. Of the 73 abusers the police have identified, 23 are currently behind bars in various prisons in Provence.

On the 17th March, my father was questioned again about the photos of myself, now dated to July 2020, and those of my two sisters-in-law. He had posted them online with his usual obscene commentary. He sticks to his denials: he had succumbed to a 'temptation to see what was hidden' but had never felt any sexual attraction to any of us.

I make an appointment to consult the full dossier at the lawyer's office.

Monday, 26th April 2021

David, Mum and I spend five long hours listening to our lawyer as she runs through the statements from the most recent batch of arrests.

Their ages run from 22 to 71. They all claim to be aficionados of candaulism – a sexual practice that involves watching your partner have sex with someone else.

The transcripts of recent interviews with my father are as insufferable as ever. When asked about the sexual assaults on my mother, he either lies or avoids giving direct answers. I no longer have any hope of discovering the truth about what he did to me.

Caty tells us there are photos of my mother tied and bound on her bed that she would rather not show us. We are thunderstruck. Treading gently, she admits that there is now good reason to believe that the rapes started earlier than previously thought – the first is now dated to the 23rd of July 2011, when they still lived in the Paris region.

My mother says nothing. Hit by a metaphorical bus for the umpteenth time, she simply switches off. There's no other way to describe it. She sits there like a waxwork, no sign of life, utterly devastated. I sit next to her, peering into a well of shame.

Sunday, 23rd May 2021

Along with Pierre and Tom, we spend the weekend with friends who live in Lyon. Mum is still quite fragile. Every day she asks herself if she really has the strength to pursue the case to the bitter end. I'm terrified by the thought that she might pull out.

This morning, Florian sends me a copy of a letter he received a few days earlier. It's dated the 22nd April:

> My son.
>
> I haven't written to anyone in the family since I've been locked up, but I've given it a lot of thought and I've chosen you because yours is the only address I have and because I think that your artist's sensibility will, I hope, let you pass on these words. They'll be

my last, which is only right with regard to you all. I understand your silence. I'll serve out my time in prison. I'll make it on my own, out of respect for you.

I'm sorry for the harm I've done you all, I ask for your pardon and you all have my excuses. I did the best I could with my personality up until these last dark years.

I think about you all, and all that's going on that I catch on the TV. I miss you all terribly. I hope your lives are full of joy and beauty. I miss all the kids, even though I've never met the most recent.

It's probably for the best.

Know that your mum is, and always will be, the love of my life and, like you all, I'll never forget her. I know how much harm I've done you and the shame I've brought you. I'm doing my best to get better here. Losing my freedom is easier to bear than your absence. I hope you took my car, it'll be useful. I hope you're all happy and full of strength. I'm getting older and my health's not so good, but that's nothing next to what I've inflicted on you all. I'll try to find the courage to keep going on my own. I love you and send you all a kiss.

Forgive me, Dad.

N.B. I've only got your address – it was on the divorce papers I was given to sign.

I read the letter three times, both bitter and sad. Could this request for forgiveness be in any way sincere? How can you hope to make us believe you have feelings for us, your children, when you ground us up and spat us out so willingly?

Nausea engulfs me.

Monday, 31st May 2021

My mother goes to the divorce court in Carpentras for the first encounter with the civil judge. My father remains in prison, and is only present on a screen. It's the first time she has seen him since he was locked up. He's haggard, stooped, much thinner. He averts his gaze.

One day, maybe, I'll talk to you for the very last time. I'll look you straight in the eyes and tell you how you threw all our lives devastatingly off course.

Life goes on for us since the 2nd November 2020, but haltingly. We march as best we can to the drum of the judicial proceedings. There's still a long way to go, and we'll be exhausted by the end.

Today, Monday the 31st May, Mum told me she'd

seen you on a large video screen in that soulless room in the Carpentras courthouse.

You, shrunken, behind bars; her, as upright as she can manage given the weight of the past she has still not shaken off. All that's left of what was once a vivacious, flamboyant couple.

Mum was shocked when she saw you for the first time after seven months' detention.

I imagine your days are difficult. You're a changed man. Or maybe you're now the man you always secretly were – without substance, lost, empty-eyed.

You told her you were sorry. That you're ashamed. We know all about shame, Dad. It's baked into us now. The hardest thing for us, your children, is to admit that we never knew who you were.

You – whom we thought a good, honest, loyal man – betrayed us, choosing to sacrifice us to your dark side, thinking you were smart enough to play by your own rules and not get caught.

Who on earth are you, deep down inside? No doubt I'll never know.

Just as we'll probably never know just how far you were willing to follow your perverse instincts. We can only assume, based on your photos and videos, that you were fundamentally corrupt, demoniac. I keep telling myself that you must have lost all love and respect for us a long, long time ago in order to be able to inflict such horrors upon us. You demolished the one family you had, giving no thought to how much we might prize it.

I loved you and respected you. I helped you, as any daughter would have who felt grateful towards her father.

You never kept up your end of the bargain. You refused to be a real father or grandfather. I'll never be able to forgive you.

And that's just something I have to learn to live with.

Monday, 23rd August 2021

My mother is with me in my little holiday home. I help her unpack, hoping that the neutral space will help her renew her zest for life. She's spent the past nine months living with her children, hopping from one to the other, but now she wants to live on her own. She feels ready.

The summer has been yet another ordeal for us, as we continue to mourn our life *before*. Although my father is still alive, we deal every day with his absence, his disappearance.

Helping Mum succeed in starting a new life is the priority now. We go shopping, we buy new things, we change the décor, we put her mark on the house, beginning with her maiden name on the letter box. It's a sign of rebirth. We laugh a lot, celebrating every completed task as a minor victory. We rearrange the furniture and alter the blinds to let in more light. Anything it takes to make her feel at home and free of spirit. We tell each other that, so long as we look out for each other, things can only get better.

The news reaches us that 34 men are now behind bars – one of them lived only a few streets away from my parents. She remembers him coming to the house on at least two separate occasions under the pretext of purchasing some bike wheels, which probably never existed.

Revolted, I read through the psychological profiles of these men. Most of them admit the amoral nature of what they did, but not one expresses any regret or empathy for my mother. Most are blithely unaware that they're dangerous criminals.

Saturday, 4th September 2021

It'll soon be time to go back to school. We sit down with Tom to evaluate how well he is coping.

Should he keep seeing the psychologist? In the course of the summer, he told us he was feeling better and wanted to stop his chats with the doctor. He seemed to have succeeded in putting some distance between himself and the emotions that tortured him. Pierre and I told him it was up to him.

Today, when I remind him of what he'd said, Tom eventually admits he'd like the therapy to continue. He says he still has things to talk over and wants to keep his weekly appointment – what he calls 'my time for me' and 'my little space'.

Wednesday, 29th September 2021

For several days now, the media – regional and national – have been circling around the case, hungry for drama. A number of apparently well-informed journalists seem to wait for the next wave of arrests – which should involve nine men – to let fly. Our story is about to be tossed into the public arena. We await the intrusion with trepidation.

In anticipation, I ask Caty to make a public statement about domestic chemical submission, a practice far more common than generally thought, and one that most women, even doctors, know little about. Shining a light on the subject is a matter of urgency. Some of the lawyers retained by the accused have already started to hint at a defence strategy: they're going to claim their clients were unaware of Mum's true state when they carried out their acts. An argument as outrageous as it is despicable.

Now that the media is heating up, we are considering opening up a new front to the case. Can we bring an action against the free hookup site used by all these perverts to communicate with each other? Many of them insist that they were innocent victims led astray by my manipulative father, and yet they all logged onto the unmoderated chat site *Coco.gg* to consult pornographic images of my visibly unconscious mother. Not one of them thought this was a cause for concern, or that they should steer well clear of my father. Quite the opposite, in fact…

Monday, 4th October 2021

A little respect for all my mum, my brothers and myself have gone through these past 11 months is not a lot to ask, surely? Apparently, it is, given the way the gutter press is playing fast and loose with details of our private lives. If compassion is too much to ask for, what about simple professionalism? Can't a minute's thought be given to the families of victims and the suffering inflicted upon them?

As I read the coverage this evening, I am scandalised. The way the case is portrayed – the headlines, the photos, the captions, the choice of vocabulary – reveals a sleazy curiosity and lewd delight, rendering any claim to professional ethics simply absurd. The journalists dip into the trough with their speculations, extrapolations, and hunger for salacious detail, before stepping back, wiping their chins and congratulating themselves on their table manners. I had no idea a press card absolved its bearers from such a multitude of sins.

These obscene scribblings have nothing in common with the writing that has kept me afloat these past months. I try, as best I can, to form words into phrases in order to guide me through this ordeal. I write to heal, to peel off all trace of my father, to free myself from the burden he has bequeathed me.

Thursday, 14th October 2021

On the 6th October, my two sisters-in-law were interviewed by the investigating magistrate in Avignon. My father was last questioned in July, as evasive and unconvincing as ever. He has never stopped trying to twist reality into something more accommodating for him. Luckily, the judge doesn't seem to give much credit to his ravings.

I've been living with my mother for several days now. My friend Marion – who's had my back from day one – rode down with me.

I came to keep my mother's spirits up and for a simple, practical reason: I've brought her a car, so that she can come and go freely. She's no longer scared to drive, since she no longer has to worry about losing consciousness behind the wheel or forgetting where she's been and what she's done.

Caty calls to tell me that one of the accused from the most recent series of rapes of my mother, dating back to the 22nd October 2020, is HIV-positive. I start to shake. Mum sees that something is up, but says nothing. I'll have to take her for a blood test next week.

With each revelation, my hatred for my father ratchets up a notch. I tell myself over and over that a single exposure doesn't guarantee HIV. But if my mother has been contaminated, I'll make sure my father pays a terrible price.

Thursday, 21st October 2021

The test is negative. Mum doesn't have HIV. I can breathe again.

Later, Mum tells me that she wasn't too worried. She simply counted on her lucky star. That she can still be so innocent, so detached, astonishes me.

We couldn't be more different in the way we cope with these extraordinary circumstances.

Saturday, 23rd October 2021

A rift has opened between my mother and myself. The family is starting to tear apart again.

Out of the blue, we've had news about my father. Florian has heard from Charles, one of his childhood friends, who now lives down south. Charles knows my parents, having been on holiday with us several times when we were all young. He recently decided to change careers and is training to become a social worker. During an internship in the prison system, he came across my father. With the obligatory mask across his face, my father didn't recognise him. Charles did, however, and what he saw came as a shock. He says my father looked transformed, lost, hollowed out. He didn't dare tell him who he was.

The news of this encounter marks what is almost the

one-year anniversary of my father's arrest. It creates waves amongst us.

As the legal proceedings drag on, my mother is increasingly convinced that my father should be given more help, better care. Sometimes she criticises me for being too virulent towards him, ungrateful even.

'You're forgetting that he wasn't always the devil incarnate. He did so much for you. For your brothers too. I was happy with him by my side. I loved him so much. I want to remember the good times. Obsessing about the rest won't do me any good. I want to enjoy life. That's my way.'

I see this as a form of armour, a way to protect herself from the brutal facts. But listening to her speaking like this leaves me feeling uncomfortable.

Wednesday, 17th November 2021

I wake up to the thought that this text will be published one day. I'm ready for it, but am conscious that, no matter how far I've come in my struggle to patch myself back together, there's still a long way to go. Key questions remain to be answered: How will my family react to this book? What will my son think, many years from now, when he's old enough to read it?

A little over a year ago, a mine exploded beneath our feet, scarring and scattering us. But we still have to piece ourselves back together and face what's yet to come. We have to stand up tall and proud, despite the pain, the disillusion, the hatred. I'm convinced that, by bearing witness, I can show that we're not the ones who should hang our heads with shame. My one hope is that this book will help others who have been abused and manipulated to rise up too.

Monday, 22nd November 2021

The investigating magistrate calls me in again, almost a year after our initial encounter. My case has to be looked over once more in the light of new elements unearthed by the enquiry. According to my lawyer, they've found more pictures taken without my knowledge. This time I'm completely naked. The judge wants to show them to me and hear what I have to say about my father's most recent declarations. I don't know what to expect. Or what state I'll be in once the interview is over. It's hard to escape the feeling of being caught up in an unending nightmare. I just want to wake up.

Eleven in the morning in the Avignon court building. The judge's office hasn't changed: same vast room, same furnishings, same staff, same Plexiglas screen between us. Several coloured folders lie on the table.

'Before we start, I'd like to know how you've been since our first interview. Is there anything you'd like to discuss before we move on to the new elements that concern you?'

'I'm worried about my mother's mental health. She seems unaware of my father's Machiavellian nature. She doesn't seem to have grasped the full extent of what he did to her down the years. I think she's still in denial, even though she's had no contact with him for the past year. She still holds him in a certain esteem, and wants to hang on to her image of him as a man who loved her, a man who once had a moral compass. She can't accept the reality, can't admit that my father deliberately manipulated her, debasing her and putting her life in danger at the same time. I think she knows that the moment she faces the truth, she will collapse. Because of this, our relationship is very complicated right now. It's going to be a long and hard slog for her – first to accept, then to heal. It pains me to see her holding reality at arm's length.'

The judge notes everything down.

'My lawyer recently showed me a letter that my aunt – my father's sister – sent to my father on the 8th September 2021. She's over 80, and is the only person in the family to have maintained contact with him. In her letter, she tells him where my mother is currently living, which is supposed to be a secret. She insists that my mother "is doing well".

As I've just told you, I couldn't agree less. My mother just wants to hang on to whatever remnants of her life *before* she can still grasp. She wants to believe that her relationship with her husband was sincere, real.'

The judge pushes on with the agenda.

'I'm going to show you images from a video made by your father where he compares photos of you and your mother. You should know that this video was shared online with other men.'

She lays down a sheet of small colour photos. One of them shows me getting dressed in the violet bedroom in their house in Mazan. I can date the photos precisely. In July 2020, I worked from my parents' home for ten days so that they could enjoy their grandson's company after six months of Covid-induced separation. I study the images for a long time. He has paired images of me with photos of my mother. He captured us both in a variety of poses – from the front, the back and the side. Beneath the images I discover his vile commentary.

I hear him in my head giving voice to his obscene words, his tone sarcastic. I grip the arms of the chair to stop myself fainting.

'It's definitely me. He must have put his phone in camera mode and hidden it under the bedside table. How could he do such a thing?!'

> I remember the summer of 2008 in Tizzano, in Corsica. You and Mum were so happy, as much in love as when you first met. Your camera never leaves your hands. You take photos of Mum incessantly.

The court recorder taps away mechanically as I speak, her eyes on her laptop. The judge has a question for me:

'When I ask your father if he has ever felt sexual desire for you, his answer is: "No, never. And if you want to know why I filmed her naked, it's just curiosity – I just wanted to lift the veil." He categorically denies having drugged you or sexually abused you. What do you think?'

'I'm convinced he did. He can't speak without lying. The two photos where I'm supposed to be asleep prove that he drugged me. I've told you before – I've never gone to bed dressed that way, and I never sleep in that position. Plus, I'm a light sleeper. For ten years I've lived with a man who gets up at quarter to two in the morning to go to work, and I've never slept through it. The slightest thing is enough to wake me up.'

I ask to look again at the photospread comparing my mother and me.

'I look a lot like my mother. It's something he's brought up time and again. I know now that he's never had the slightest respect for the mother of his children. And look at these comments – he always refers to me as my mother's daughter, not his, not theirs. He's dissociating himself from his existence as father. And why? Because he sees us nothing more than sexual objects.'

'Now,' says the judge, 'I'd like you to try to recall where you were during the night of the 27th and 28th December 2019.'

'After Christmas, Pierre and Tom and I went off to Morocco. We stayed there until the 2nd January. My parents stayed in our house while we were away.'

The judge shows me another photo of my mother, undressed and unconscious.

'This is the least shocking of this particular series of photos taken by your father. Could it have been taken in your home while you were away?'

My mother lies on her left side, as in all the other photos of her in a drugged state. All she wears are black lace panties. Definitely not her normal style. The bedside light is on, as is the ceiling lamp. He hasn't bothered to take off her ankle boots. I recognise the bedroom. It's mine. My house. My special place.

'Madame Darian, on this particular night your mother was raped for several hours in your house by a 34-year-old man she'd never met. Your father filmed the whole thing. Mobile phone tower records show that both their phones were active in the zone of your house at nine minutes to eleven at night.'

My lawyer had warned me this was coming but, even so, I'm not sure I can take another punch to the gut like this. How could he carry out such a barbarous act in the intimacy of my house? How can I ever feel at home within its walls ever again? How will Pierre react?

'I'm afraid there's more, madame Darian. I have another photo of your mother, unconscious, to show you. It was taken somewhere else.'

If there had been a pause button, I would have hit it. But there isn't.

The photo shows my mother in exactly the same pose, inert, on her left side, her mouth open. Once again, she's been trussed up in vulgar, ugly, degrading black underwear.

It's my room, my bed, my sheets, but it's not my house outside Paris. This photo was taken in my holiday home. I feel crushed, have difficulty breathing. My vision and hearing are troubled. The photo was taken on the night of the 6th May 2019, when my mother was raped for five hours straight.

I can no longer ignore how horrific the court proceedings to come will be, for both my mother and myself. I cannot bear to think that strangers used my home to abuse her. I fight the urge to vomit.

The judge asks whether I think a face-to-face encounter with my father might help me in some way. The doctor who carried out my court-mandated psychological analysis has suggested it.

'I would be present, if it's something you want to do,' she tells me. 'You could ask him any questions that you might have, and tell him what you feel, what you've been through.'

'He's of no interest to me anymore. His whole life has been a tissue of lies and monstrosities. The next time I see my father, it will be when I come to the courtroom to hear the verdict.'

I ask the judge if any other victims have been identified in the case. She informs me that my father raped another woman a dozen times between 2015 and 2020. She, too, had been put under. The woman's partner had received the necessary drugs from my father beforehand, complete with instructions for their use. However, the victim in question does not wish to pursue charges against either abuser. She has forgiven her husband and writes to him regularly while he is held in jail. Everything indicates that her husband has somehow managed to maintain his iron hold over this poor woman. His case is still being examined by the prosecutor's office in Avignon.

The last thing the judge tells me is that one of the men arrested has requested that he and my mother be questioned together. He asserts that she consented to the abuse, that she had waved him into her bedroom. My mother has agreed to the request, refusing to be intimidated or leave such an obvious lie unchallenged. The joint interview is scheduled to take place in a few months.

Thanks to the remarkable work of the investigative team and all the experts they have mobilised, 47 men in all have been brought in for questioning. Forty-five have been charged and placed in custody. Of those, one died shortly after being arrested, two have subsequently been released and two have agreed to testify for the prosecution. I wait impatiently for those who abused my mother for years on end to be tried and condemned.

Sunday, 28th November 2021

This is my last entry in this chronicle of horror and survival. The writer Maurice Pinguet once said: 'To write is to enter the dark night we all carry within us.' That night certainly lurks within me, a dense, cold darkness willed upon me by my father. Writing this book hasn't made it disappear, but it has helped me to explore its extent, mapping it out to master my fear of the unknown. It's not easy for a victim of this kind of crime to expose her inner feelings. Confronting the torments of this terrible moment has required all my strength. Confronting myself was no easier, but has done me the world of good: I have found my centre of gravity and am ready to confront the trials to come, along with my mum and my brothers.

Finding the right words is therapeutic. It has helped me to bind my wounds and identify possible ways forward. I have no idea how the world will react to my account, but I am sure of one thing: this is only the beginning of my fight for women and their causes.

Mum will undoubtedly be called in again and again by the judge from here to the trial. Every time, the dark night will engulf us again, full of echoes from our life *before*.

With 50-odd men behind bars, the investigation has still a long and difficult path to follow. Some of the men who raped my mother will be condemned – young single men, fathers with kids, grandfathers. Some may never be caught. We know that at least 70 men abused her over a ten-year period, some of them repeatedly. How have we managed to live alongside these sexual predators and remain blind to their deeds? The same question, to an even greater degree, can be asked about the instigator, the organiser, the conductor of it all, the man in whom we placed our trust, whose mind and heart we never doubted.

The trial is scheduled for 2024 in a courtroom in the south of France. Mum will be over 70 by then. Will she have the strength to face it, even with the love and support of her children, through a trial that take months to resolve? I try to find solace in the fact that she would still, at this very moment, be caught up in a far worse ordeal had my father not been caught in that supermarket on the 2nd November 2020.

I'm determined to overcome my appalling paternal heritage, like an alchemist coaxing gold from the basest material. Society must help women and children who have been crushed by sexual violence. So much remains to be done in France to help and protect the victims of sexual abuse and assault who have the courage to file charges. The current psychological support system is completely inadequate. It is sluggish, insufficient; its workings are random and unpredictable. Not all victims receive the same level of help, the most vulnerable least of all.

I want this book to sound the alarm about the prevalence of chemical submission in France and around the world. The general public must be made aware that the practice goes far beyond date-rape cocktails in night clubs. Everyone should take a wary look inside their medicine cabinet: anti-anxiety drugs, sleeping pills and a host of other mind-altering substances have been used as arms of sexual assault. It is an epidemic that touches all social classes. Regular memory lapses should set alarm bells ringing. If it happens to you, tell your doctor and ask for toxicology screening.

By the time 2024 comes around and the trial begins, will society have woken up to this problem? The organisations currently committed to this fight are too few and too underfunded. The victims are faced not only with the terror of their situation, and fear of repercussions, but with a suffocating sense of culpability and shame. My mother is guilty of nothing, and has nothing to be ashamed about. The same is true for every other victim out there. Faced with the unthinkable, the unbearable, we must fight back.

This is the end of Caroline Darian's original book, *I'll Never Call Him Dad Again*. What follows is her second book, published in France as *Pour Que L'On Se Souvienne*, or *Lest We Forget*. For this edition, the two books have been combined.

Monday, 2nd September 2024

The first day of the trial will stay with me for the rest of my days.

The feminist demonstrators who had gathered to welcome us before the doors of the courthouse could be seen and heard from far away: 'Rapists – we see you! Victims – we believe you!'

We arrive: my mother in front, her children behind her, our lawyers by our side. My three childhood friends are there to support me. We enter the courthouse, clear security, cross the harshly lit main hall, and enter the crowded courtroom, where photographers elbow camera crews, blinding us with their flashes. Taking the lead from Gisèle, who had the final say, the entire family requests that all measures of confidentiality be lifted and that the trial take place in public view. Our lawyers add their voices to ours. Much to our surprise, our application causes the trial to be immediately suspended at the request of the state prosecutor and some of the defence lawyers. We have turned standard practice on its head. Rape trials are normally confidential to protect the victims, but we're convinced that, on this occasion, the accused would be the only ones to benefit. Our lawyers hammer home our position: 'It's time for shame to change sides.' That phrase had become our slogan. Thirty minutes go by. The presiding judge, Roger Arata, accepts our request: 'The proceedings will be public.'

Looking back, the significance of this decision cannot be overstated as it rendered the trial into an event that would make history. At the time, it was not an easy call. In his closing remarks, the chief prosecutor admitted he had been hesitant at first: 'We initially asked for a confidential trial as a protective measure. But we underestimated your strength of character, which the violence of the crimes you suffered had only served to reinforce. Yours was the right choice, Mrs Pelicot.'

Opting for a public trial was no easy matter for the family. The same was true of our decision to insist that the sordid videos be projected in the courtroom to drive home the truth of what had taken place. Of course we hesitated. Of course we were plagued by doubt. Were we making a big mistake? Would our audacious choice be understood? Would it serve any positive purpose?

After the fact, we know the answer to that final question: yes, a hundred times yes.

The trial's opening day offers me the first glimpse of my father since his arrest. I watch him enter the glass-walled dock. Sandwiched between two police officers, his eyes are furtive, his manner subdued. He clutches a stick, moving awkwardly on unsteady legs. Although his hair is whiter and his face bleary with age, he remains as I remembered him and not the shrunken, withered figure I had expected. My heart and stomach clench as I look at him. I want to cry, but I mustn't and I won't. To my left, I hear a sharp intake of breath before my mother murmurs: 'My God, he looks like Joseph, his grandfather on his mother's side … He's turned into his grandfather.'

Eight metres separate us; a gap too big for any words. All we can do is exchange glances. An imaginary conversation immediately kicks off in my head. I wish we could open up to each other like we did *before*. I want to talk to my father. I have so much to say to him, so much to beg of him. I'm in so much pain; the wound he inflicted four years previously hasn't healed, but I refuse to let it be seen. I fix him with a cold, accusing glare, trembling in my seat but refusing to flinch. The trial will be long, and I have to be ready for a war of attrition.

He is soon joined by the 17 co-accused who, like him, haven't left prison since being arrested. The 33 others, those on bail, are bunched together less than a metre from us. They seem to lock eyes with us. The pocket-sized courtroom in which the proceedings will play out leaves us exposed, jammed up tight against them. A proximity that will last four months. Studying their postures and expressions, I notice that they cover the entire spectrum of French society: not just the pitifully marginal petty crooks and strutting troublemakers but also the serious and respectable. A crowd of photographers unleash a barrage of flashes before the judges enter and the opening statements begin. For almost ten minutes, all I can hear are shutters clicking.

Finally, we hear the bell signalling the start of the proceedings. The photographers fall back, taking their electrical storm with them, and the judges file in. Standing to mark their entrance will soon become an instinctive response, but on this occasion, there is a certain solemnity. My eyes seek out Dominique, to catch him with his back against the wall. He can no longer dodge and weave. The time has come for him to face up to the depravity of his acts.

The accused are called forward one by one, beginning with Dominique. He gets up from his chair, leans unsteadily over the microphone in his glassed-in compartment and states his identity, his profession, his marital status and his place of residence. It's been a long time since I've heard his voice. I'm surprised by the harsh, stifled tones. His speech used to be clear and confident, even brash, but now it's almost inaudible, the voice of a broken old man. Or, at least, that's what he'd like us to think.

One after another, the accused state their names, like children on the first day of school. Ironically, this is my son Tom's first day back at school – usually a big day for both of us. I should be with him, but I'm here watching this dismal spectacle. I've been wrenched from his life and that of everyone else I know.

Each of the accused must enter a plea: will they accept the charges laid against them and admit full responsibility? Only 14 of the 51 plead guilty to raping Gisèle, and only a tiny number of those show any visible remorse.

This beginning in and of itself leaves me sick to my stomach. It is the first indication that the accused are beyond contempt, ready to plumb any depths in the hope of shrugging off all traces of guilt.

Tuesday, 3rd September 2024

The second day, of so many to come, proves no easier. The presiding judge announces he will present the charge sheet for each of the 51 accused. Kicking off at 9.15 a.m., he indicates that he will not plough through each and every word of the interminable list of alleged crimes but rather present a summary highlighting the key points to be presented before the court. This can only mean he will focus on what is most difficult for us to bear, and I automatically shift to a more distant mindset, reaching for whatever protective armour I possess.

I close my eyes, empty my mind, and concentrate on just getting through. I already know every sordid detail of the dossiers compiled by the prosecution. This is the moment when the worst of what my family has endured will be set out for public display. Words – depending on how they are chosen and how they are delivered – can be harder to bear than images. My mother remains imperturbable, her back ramrod straight, her legs crossed. We flank her, as do Anne-Sophie and Candice, two psychologists from a victim support association. They will watch over us during the four months of the trial. Their expert advice and simple kindness, palpable in their every look and gesture, will help us overcome the horrors of what is to come – Dominique's heartlessness, the insults of the co-accused and the shameless pleading of the defence lawyers.

It takes the judge several hours to describe the innumerable sexual assaults endured by Gisèle, rape after barbarous rape. Each phrase he utters crushes my heart a little more. His description of acts beyond reason, beyond decency, leave me nauseous. The accessories chosen by Gisèle's torturers were crude and absurd; the acts perpetrated on her fragile body were inhuman. How could Dominique have humiliated her to such an extent? Much of what is said is literally unimaginable – it is almost impossible to believe that such hellish abuses actually took place. And yet they did.

Gisèle never wavers, sitting stolidly through it all, apparently impervious to all she hears. Once again, I am astonished by her stoic endurance.

The judge reaches the part about me. He talks of the photos taken without my knowledge, the file on the hard drive named 'My naked daughter', and the ever-shifting statements made by Dominique on the subject over the past two and half years. I cannot move. The silence of the courtroom echoes around me. I start to shake. Try as I might, I cannot stifle my cries of distress. Every time I think of these images, I feel betrayed and besmirched. Listening to another person summarise the facts in a clear and authoritative tone convinces me once again that the worst undoubtedly happened. I stagger precipitously out of the courtroom, unable to stand the public humiliation, and collapse onto a bench in the hall.

The trauma I felt on the 3rd November 2020, when I was first shown the two photos in the police station in Carpentras, rushes back. I seize up, my muscles contracting painfully. I am frozen with horror and grief. My brother Florian comes to my rescue, as he did back then too, followed by Anne-Sophie, the psychologist. They conceal me from onlookers in a little enclosure in the centre of the hall and help me overcome the spasms that follow. It takes twenty minutes or so for me to steady myself, during which time the session has been suspended. My lawyer comes to ask me if I want to return to the courtroom to listen to the rest of the charges or whether I'd rather spare myself and leave for the day. I don't want to run away, so I force myself to go back in.

Wednesday, 4th September 2024

The third day starts with a debate over whether the videos, which provide irrefutable proof of the hundreds of rapes endured by my mother, should be shown. Then the defence lawyers take the floor to respond to the charges brought against their clients.

As far as I'm concerned, nothing they have to say deserves to be heard. Their clients raped and sullied Gisèle, in some cases repeatedly. Full stop. End of debate.

The defence lawyers seem intent on competing to see who can be the lowest of the low. The presiding judge, Roger Arata, does nothing to stop them. I am shocked by the lack of common decency on display. Guillaume de Palma explains to the court: 'There's rape, and then there's rape.' Nadia El Bouroumi prefaces a remark with the words:

'While Mrs Pelicot gave my client a blowjob…' Isabelle Crépin-Dehaene insists that my mother is actually a sexual exhibitionist. They push me to breaking point once again. This is reality to me – I can't dismiss their shameless remarks and virulent attacks as mere rhetorical flourishes.

For a second time, I leave the courtroom. This time I don't go back. Even my mother will be driven to do so later in the trial, particularly when one lawyer describes a video as 'depicting a sexual game with three players' and demands that the court consider 'whether Gisèle Pelicot was not actually a willing accomplice in all that went on'.

I don't even try to keep a low profile. I rise from my seat as a deliberate act of protest. Standing up and walking out is the only recourse I'm allowed in this court, so I depart. The legal system places no limits on what can be said during criminal proceedings, no matter how degrading for the victims. But, like every other decent human being, I have my principles, and I refuse to set them aside. As I leave the courtroom, I take the time to look each and every one of the accused in the eyes. They, in return, simply size me up – just another potential sexual object.

As for Dominique, he lowers his gaze and thrusts his head into his hands – hands that now disgust me, given all they have done.

That night, my phone rings, as does my mother's. It's our lawyers, warning us about a photo found in Dominique's collection that Counsellor Isabelle Crépin-Dehaene plans to submit to the court the next day. She is convinced that it is a photo of Gisèle, and that it will prove her complicity.

It's a photo of a sadomasochistic scene featuring a woman with straight-cut auburn hair who bears some resemblance to Gisèle. She's on a sort of swing in the garage of the house in Mazan, blindfolded with her hands cuffed and her legs splayed. Needless to say, it soon becomes clear it's a different woman, one who voluntarily chose to submit to Dominique's sexual fantasies.

But this is the level of the debate we have to wade through over the next few days. We harden ourselves as the defence lawyers attempt to land one low blow after another. Faced with their vile posturing, I remain in a state of permanent disbelief, my mother in one of silent outrage.

Thursday, 5th September 2024

This is a day that stands out.

Gisèle will appear as a witness for the first time in the court. There is a scrum of media outside the courtroom, including many foreign correspondents. It is almost impossible to get through them. Gisèle is in the spotlight, all the news channels having flagged her testimony as the day's key event. There is an even longer queue than normal for the public gallery. There's a distinctive feeling in the air – a mix of anxiety, expectation and solemnity.

Gisèle is ready. She has been rehearsing for this moment for weeks. When she addresses the court, she's not allowed to use any notes. For someone so normally self-effacing, this is a huge challenge, all the more so as we are all aware of the historic nature of what she has to say.

When called to the witness stand, she rises slowly and paces steadily down the middle of the courtroom, a warrior prepared for combat. She has abandoned the dark glasses of previous days. She reveals her face so that no one – especially the accused – can ignore the facial expression that contains the horrors she was made to endure for so many years. With fierce dignity, she comes to show her wounds for all to see. And yet her perpetual elegance remains. Head high, she faces the panel of judges, adjusts the microphone and takes a sip of water. With bated breath, the courtroom awaits. Then she speaks, her voice firm, each word chosen with care. She doesn't stop until almost an hour has gone by. One of our lawyers stands to her left, shielding her from Dominique, who cannot take his eyes from her. His posture is that of a child pleading for a gift, craving a glance from her. It doesn't come. Not this time.

She begins with her childhood, her education, her mother's illness and death, the care provided by her maternal grandmother, Marie, her love for her father and her brother, Michel, who died young. She sums up this first part of the statement by saying: 'Ours was a family that shared laughter, not tears.' Then she tells of meeting Dominique and the family that came along with him, including his violent, selfish, domineering and twisted father.

When she talks of the November day when she discovered all the horrors that had been inflicted upon her, she tries to convey its impact: 'My entire world collapsed. Fifty years of my life went up in smoke.' She closes with a message for Dominique, delivered without once turning towards him: 'This is what I have to say to the man sitting to my left: I gave you everything. I tried without fail to help you find the light and the joy it brings, but you chose darkness, you preferred to bury yourself in the shadows.'

She talks of the love she bears for her three children and seven grandchildren and explains why she chose not to change her name, remaining Gisèle Pelicot for the trial so that a shred of something noble might attach itself to the family name alongside the infamy brought by her tormentor.

She mentions my book and admits that she thought its publication should have been delayed, but that she respected my choice to go ahead. She talks of her admiration for the non-profit organisation I founded, Don't Put Me Under, and how proud she is of all the time and energy I have committed to the pursuit of its goals.

Addressing the tactics of the defence lawyers, she takes them to task for all she has been forced to listen to over the past days, their talk of sex games, of libertines, of swinging couples: 'I don't want to hear any more talk about sexual practices. There are no sex scenes in this case, only rape scenes. I've never had a threesome, I've never participated in wife-swapping, I've never been a swinger. I had no part in any of this. I never agreed to it. I never pretended to be asleep.'

Her words for the accused are simple and direct: 'For once in your life, take responsibility for what you have done.' And then she closes with a declaration: 'Today I'm taking my life back. Today I denounce the practice of chemical submission.'

After a few questions from her own counsel, Gisèle faces the attacks of the defence lawyers, who try in vain to twist her words. For the greater part of the day, she has to stand there and listen to their mocking questions, their deliberately ambiguous phrases and double meanings, and their unscrupulous needling.

At the close of the session, the presiding judge announces he will suspend the projection of the videos of the rapes while the objections of the defence lawyers are heard.

It takes eight days of legal argument to defeat their pleas and win the right for the truth to be shown in all its horror.

Friday, 6th September 2024

It's my turn to take the stand, along with my sisters-in-law, Céline and Aurore.

It's one of the worst experiences of my life. I mustn't collapse or give in to my rage. I have to be calm and reserved while I run through all I have to say, not so much to the court but to Dominique himself. During the past few weeks, I've tried time and again to write down the key points of my testimony to memorise so that I forget nothing when in the line of fire. But I decide in the end to be spontaneous, to seize the moment of truth and hope that I won't let myself, or the others, down.

The presiding judge announces that only twenty minutes remain before the court will break for lunch. One of us has to step forward and claim the slot. Paralysed, I look to my two sisters-in-law to see what they'll do. Then, in a fraction of a second, I realise it has to be me. I can't put it off any longer, no matter how painful or perilous it may prove. My problem now is that I have so much to say, so much to squeeze in and so little time.

Speaking out will, at least, put an end to the emotional and physical torture of waiting. I force myself to stand up. As I cross the courtroom, my palms are sweaty and my heart is pounding, but my gaze remains steady as it sweeps across the ranks of the accused and their lawyers.

I take the stand, my hands grasping each other. I squeeze them together, my knuckles white, in the hope that the tension will ripple back up through my spine and help me stand straight. Dominique is only two metres to my left. I fix my eyes on his and keep them there for what seems an eternity, although it can only have been a few seconds. I brush aside the fact that he appears to be on the verge of tears. I won't let him steal the spotlight. Not here. Not now. It's my turn to be seen and heard.

Roger Arata asks me to state my identity. There is compassion in his face. He is due to retire soon. This will be his last major trial. For me, it's my last chance to convince Dominique to finally confess to everything he has done.

My voice and my body tremble, but my words pour forth.

'At 8.25 p.m. on the 2nd November 2020, I was torn from one life and thrown into another when my mother told me: "I spent most of the day in the police station. Your father's been drugging me and raping me, along with a host of other men." Instinctively, I called my brothers, who were just as lost, just as tearful, just as confused. We were all in a state of shock. The next day, I discovered that my father had taken naked photos of me without my knowledge. I can't come to terms with it. Close-ups of my most intimate parts have been posted to the internet and commented upon. By whom? Where are those images now? Where will they be five, ten years down the line? My child, and all his cousins, have had their innocence torn from them. Not only has my son lost a grandfather, but the grandfather he thought he had was a complete fabrication.' I end with a plea to the judges, whose sympathy is apparent in their rapt silence: 'How do you rise from such a bed of ashes?'

After lunch it was Céline's turn to take the stand. She married my brother David some twenty years ago. She had been very fond of Dominique, who embraced her as a new daughter. David and Céline's kids are the eldest of my parents' grandchildren. Being the ones who had stayed the most often with their grandparents and spent the most time with Dominique, they suffered the most when the revelations came to light. I know what she will tell the court: how distressed she has been as both a wife and mother; how her life has been upended; how everything she knew has been swept away by the tidal wave of horror.

Céline was with David when Gisèle called him on the 2nd November 2020. She watched him grow pale, rush to the toilet to vomit, pull himself together and organise, with my husband Pierre's invaluable support, our immediate travel to Mazan. She set out to protect her children from the bombshell as best she could. At first, she told them David had to rush down to their grandmother's without explaining why. But her eldest son, Nathan, soon realised that something was seriously wrong and demanded an explanation. She struggled to find the right words for a 14-year-old – 'Your grandfather has been imprisoned because he did something very bad to your grandmother.' As time went on, she was obliged to explain about the drugs, the rapes, the photos. Before long, it was Nathan who needed his parents' love and attention as he shared disturbing memories of being touched by Dominique, of being forced to play doctor and patient, of being pulled into hugs and made to take showers in his presence. They're still working to help him overcome this trauma. When he said he wanted to file a criminal complaint, they were with him every step of the way.

Céline has shocking discoveries of her own to share with the court. In March 2021, she was called in to a police station to discover a dozen photos taken of her in her bathroom by Dominique. She was also shown in photoshopped images with two men, labelled with obscene comments. She had to wait until the eve of the trial to learn that there were actually one hundred photos of her, taken in her own home across many years, in the bedroom and bathroom, many of them while she was pregnant with twins. She shares her fears with the court: how long was the period during which he had clandestinely photographed her? How many images are there? Are they all over the dark web? Had he done the same with her children when they spent the holidays with their grandparents? Could he have drugged them? The day her children found Gisèle in her bedroom in Mazan, seemingly asleep but really out cold and completely unresponsive, had he done the same to them the previous night so that he would have a free rein for his abuse of Gisèle?

So many questions without answers. So much pain for her and her children.

She speaks of the weight she has gained, the alopecia she has suffered, feeling estranged from her own body, her sleepless nights, and the exhaustion and loss of concentration that have undermined her professional life.

The betrayal, on such a private and personal level, has shattered her confidence, scarred her son, and unmoored her twin daughters.

Aurore steps up after Céline to explain how she, Florian and their children were devastated by the unfolding events. For her, the experience reopened old wounds, due to her history of childhood abuse by her own grandfather. She explains how her daughters hesitated to tell her about a game their grandfather invented – if they lifted up their T-shirts in the supermarket with him, he would give them sweets. She talks of the guilt she suffers because she'd had an intuitive feeling, years before everything had been revealed, that something was wrong, but she had been too afraid to voice her suspicions. At a time when she and Florian lived in the same house as Dominique and Gisèle, she had overheard Dominique ask then four-year-old Nathan in his bedroom: 'But why don't you want to play doctor and patient?' Afraid to awaken the demons of the abuse she had herself suffered, she had remained on the other side of the bedroom door, uncertain of what to say or do, repeating to herself that she was now in a safe place, in a family where such evil was inconceivable.

Dominique's unprecedented crimes have torn apart every branch of the family, crushing each and every one of us. It has taken us a long time to put words to our suffering, to move towards a shared understanding, to start piecing ourselves back together. We're still only part of the way there.

Monday, 9th September 2024

In the second week of the trial, a clinical assessment of Dominique's personality is presented to the court, pieced together by both a medical doctor and a psychological expert. But it is the expert testimony of another doctor, Paul Bensussan, which deeply affects me and stays with me. In the preceding weeks, I had suffered several sleepless nights after receiving a copy of his report. It confirmed, with clinical precision, all I suspected. It contained Dominique's answers to those who had grilled him about the photos he'd taken of me: 'I wanted to compare her body to her mother's. Was my curiosity a little perverse? Sure. I can't explain it, other than to say I did it because I wanted to do it.' The doctor's assessment was pitiless: 'It is clear that he just makes things up as he goes along. If you compare one interview to the next, there are always breaks in continuity … Whatever love he might claim for those close to him, it has never been strong enough to stop him acting on his impulses.'

Doctor Bensussan presents his conclusions to the court, insisting on Dominique's complex and contradictory personality. He suggests that lies underpin Dominique's entire being: lies he believed he could reconcile with life as a perfect husband, father and grandfather. Bensussan is convincing in his assertion that Dominique will never come clean to me about all he has done: 'The vigour with which Mr Pelicot defends himself, the sweeping and stubborn way he denies everything, simply illustrates how limited his capacity for empathy truly is, assuming he has any. Faced with such a personality, it is doubtful that anybody could reach him at a deep level, and almost certain that nothing would have the power to alter his cherished beliefs about himself.'

'How do you drag the truth out of a man like that?' asks Antoine Camus, one of our lawyers, hoping for a means to lead Dominique out of the labyrinth of lies and denial in which he has enclosed himself. The doctor's reply is laconic: 'God only knows.'

Friday 27th September, 2024

I go back to Paris. The first weeks of the trial and doctor Bensussan's testimony have left me drained, convinced my questions will remain unanswered, that not the slightest element of truth will be offered up, never mind a full confession. All there is are Dominique's shameless, meandering, evasive improvisations. All I can expect is a deafening silence.

Four years earlier, when I was first ambushed by the revelations about my father, I sought refuge in a psychiatric facility. Now, albeit under different circumstances, I feel the same need. After so many sleepless nights, it is imperative that I go to a quiet place to rest, to get away, to write and think about our fight with one of the worst sexual predators of the past 30 years. I need a refuge, a place I'll feel safe. A place where I can prepare myself to return to the fray and help all the other victims out there.

Tuesday, 8th October 2024

Many weeks go by before it's my husband's turn to reply to an official summons to appear as a witness. On Tuesday 8th October 2024, Pierre walks across the courtroom in his grey suit, hands burrowed deep in his pockets, a grimace carved on his face. Dominique watches his every step. Having identified himself, Pierre announces to the court: 'I was once his son-in-law, but that man no longer exists as far as I'm concerned.' He glances at Dominique. 'To tell the truth, I adored that man. There were many moments when I felt that we were incredibly close.' He explains how Dominique and Gisèle had helped him cope with the death of his mother in 2008. He pauses. 'But the worst of it is the way he betrayed my son … In November 2020, he forced me to tell a little boy, only six years old, that he couldn't see his grandfather again because he had been bad to his grandmother.'

Stoically, he describes a discussion he'd recently had with our son. 'A few weeks ago, knowing I'd soon have to do this, I asked my son if there was anything he wanted me to say to his grandfather today. At first, he said there was, but didn't say what. I thought he might want to write it down, but I received nothing from him, so I asked him why. He said: "I've changed my mind, Dad. I've nothing more to say to him."' Pierre says it again: 'This man's grandson has nothing to say to him.' In the dock, Dominique is crestfallen, his cheeks damp with tears. His eyes are fixed on Pierre's, pleading with him. Pierre doesn't give an inch: 'I don't know Dominique Pelicot, I just knew the façade he put up for public consumption.'

How could Pierre have ever imagined that his affable and respectable father-in-law, the man with whom he was so close, could do such a thing to his own daughter – take half-naked, suggestive photos of her without her knowledge while she slept? I know Pierre had been as shell-shocked as I was when he saw the images for the first time: 'I don't recognise this underwear, and I can say for sure it doesn't belong to Caroline.' He has good reason to be confident in his judgement. 'I'm the one who does the laundry in our house. I've never seen nor washed this underwear.' He insists that throughout our 20 years together, he has never seen me asleep as shown in the photos. 'There's no question about it – Caroline, my wife, was drugged. The question we should be asking is *why* he sedated her.'

'In the aftermath of these horrors, the focus of my life has been the wellbeing of my son.' He hesitates. He has something to add, although he wonders if he should. He does. 'And supporting my wife.'

The phrase appears to have slipped out against his will. It's as if the phrase had been torn from his lips. As I hear it echo around the courtroom, I realise what a toll my distress has taken on my husband. Pierre stiffens, lost in grief, his face red, his expression drawn. He tries to hold back his tears, but he can't. He grabs the side of the witness box, draws in a long, desperate breath and looks up at the ceiling – just as he did on the day of his mother's funeral, when he was called upon to say goodbye. He has suffered for four long years, watching me collapse and hide in solitude, tormented by his inability to save me. Even now he feels powerless, all too aware of the distress caused by my father's silence and constant evasion since the start of the trial.

Dominique asks to speak. He wishes to address his son-in-law. His throat is thick, and his voice is difficult to hear. 'You've always been like a son to me. None of this is your fault. The responsibility lies solely with me. I'm truly sorry for all the inconvenience I've caused in your professional and family life.' His words are, at the very least, inappropriate, if not utterly derisory. 'There's just one thing I ask you to believe: I never, ever touched my daughter or my grandchildren.'

Is this the closest he will come to a confession? Is he finally admitting that he drugged me? Despite his copious tears, like a child caught misbehaving, he adds nothing to the truth I already know deep down inside. Pierre looks away from him and sips from a glass of water.

Dominique's hand trembles. 'I don't know how, but I hope one day something will prove to you what I've just said. As for the rest, I accept full responsibility. I hope you'll accept my excuses, as that's all I can offer now. Thank you for taking the time to listen to me.'

Pierre's face remains blank. Chin up and jaw clenched, he turns without a glance at Dominique and takes the first stride that will carry him out of the courtroom.

Monday, 18th November 2024

I come back to Avignon for three days that I feel sure will prove crucial to the trial and to my future campaigning. Difficult days await us, but I feel sure that they should bring a turning point. My brothers will testify, and I will have my final opportunity to speak. After that, it will all be in the hands of the legal teams, both prosecution and defence. At court, we will gather together by our mother's side in the area reserved for the civil parties, our eyes on Dominique, clinging to the hope that at least a fragment of the truth he stubbornly denies us will come to light.

We will finally hear our lawyers plead, defending our rights, expressing our hopes, quoting our words and recalling our scars. Theirs will be the final voice demanding justice.

The second time around, it is no easier being in Avignon. I feel just as dizzy as I had in the days before the trial started. I can't walk straight, my legs give way, I can't keep anything down – all symptoms of Meniere's disease, a condition of the inner ear that I had encountered for the first time in September, but which vanished as soon as I set foot in the courthouse.

My brother David and his wife, Céline, join me in the courtroom at 10.30 a.m. The penultimate accused is being questioned. A journalist by profession, he is more at ease than the others, choosing his words with care. But his defence is as despicable as that of his fellow accused. He arrived in Mazan during the night of the 14th January 2018 expecting, so he says, a homosexual liaison. He says Dominique browbeat him into having a 'fling' with Gisèle. He is accused of aggravated rape and possession of child pornography. The only excuse he can offer is pitiful: 'My judgement was poor. I should have shown more character. It's a shame I didn't.'

Jaded, we listen to him trying to convince the court of his innocence. He proves no different from his fellow accused.

This afternoon, David, Florian and I will be called upon to speak. For weeks now, we have been anticipating this decisive moment, full of hope and fear. It will be our final opportunity to provoke Dominique into dropping his mask and speaking the truth.

David is the first to step up to the box.

He walks with ease and determination, his head held high. When he speaks, his voice is clear.

The courtroom immediately holds its breath, pregnant with expectation.

'On the 2nd November 2020, a tsunami washed away the very foundations of our family. Each of us knows where he or she was, and with whom, on that day. When I picked up the telephone and heard my mother's voice, I feared the worst – an accident, or someone gravely ill. The call barely lasted five minutes. Nothing could have been worse than what she told me. The man sitting over there had served my mother up to a horde of strangers to be raped. I spent the whole night thinking about it: "What state is she in? Is she safe?" Sleep was out of the question. I'll never forget how I felt when I saw my sister and brother on the platform of the train station the next day and during our seemingly endless journey to Mazan. Our tears. Our incomprehension. And the question that kept tormenting me: are there photos of my kids?

'Once we reached the house in Mazan, we decided that anything that connects us to this man must be destroyed. It took us two days. Photos, albums, paintings, clothes – they were all thrown away before we turned our back definitively on that house of horrors.

'One image from those days has stayed with me. We're back home. My mother is with us. All she has is one suitcase and her dog. That's all that remains from an entire life, from *before*.

'Through the weeks that followed, my mother kept going off on her own for long walks. She told me: "David, when I walk, I talk to that man. I ask him, why did he do it? What did I do to deserve it? Sometimes I scream."

'As for me, what have I lost? Who have I lost? I've lost a man who gave me a decent education, who passed on solid values, who said I had to show some backbone and stand up to the world. I've lost real companionship, our mutual passion for football, our love of cinema, a host of moments we shared together. None of that exists anymore. My parents knew how to pull a surprise birthday out of a hat. All our friends would be there, and they'd all say: "You're so lucky to have a father like yours." Everybody adored him. My friends were as dumbstruck as I was. My entire childhood has vanished, as if it never existed.

'What we ask of the court is that its decisions be aligned with our suffering. The men behind me and that man over there must be punished for the atrocities and the horror they inflicted upon our mother.

'As for you,' – he swivels towards Dominique – 'I expect you to say what you did to my sister. And to Nathan, my son.'

David pauses to gather himself. His eyes bore into Dominique as he gives voice to all his anger and revulsion. I can barely breathe. 'How could you? Tell the truth about Caroline and your grandchildren!'

Dominique barks back: 'Nothing. I did nothing to them. Never.'

Gisèle can't sit still. She can't pretend that this exchange has left her indifferent. David's words make me cry. He has had my back since the day our world collapsed. He was there when the revelations sent me into a tailspin, when I started to write, when I set out to establish Don't Put Me Under, when I needed a sympathetic ear to listen to my doubts and my despair. I know for a fact that he spent far less time than I did in mourning our father. He immediately realised the depth of Dominique's lies and the fact that we were all his prey.

Having made sure Gisèle and I were taken care of, his attention turned immediately to the children. When Nathan, his son, told him of his nightmares and shared his memories of his grandfather's words, gestures and behaviour, David and Céline immediately believed him. I've always known that David was Dominique's favourite. They even resembled each other. So much so that David used to worry about it. I knew David hoped that the love he and his father shared *before* might make him more inclined to listen to his request for Dominique to own up. Disappointment awaits him.

David makes his position crystal clear: 'I believe Caroline.'

I start sobbing. I can't bear any more lies from Dominique. I should be used to them by now, since he has repeated them day after day, but I've never been able to hear them with indifference, and I never will.

I think of Nathan, my beloved nephew, now 18 years old. We now share something that goes beyond our familial connection. Neither of us has any solid evidence to back up our status as victims. Both of us will have to wait for another trial for the things Dominique has done to us to be judged. I recall Nathan's account of the recurring flashback he's been having: he's at Mazan, seated in Dominique's red sports car as it drives towards a grocery shop, where a man with long hair gets into the car and Dominique tells Nathan to put his hand into the man's underwear or else he'll be punished. Once Aurore told Nathan what she had heard through his bedroom door all those years before, with Dominique forcing him to play doctor and patient, he opened up about all that Dominique had done to him between the ages of three and six. Thanks to his psychologist and to memories recovered through therapy and body work therapy, he has been able to detail all he suffered and pin down the date of each assault.

Nathan is still in therapy, still coming to terms with what happened to him, still dealing with his anger. He tried to write to Dominique, to put his feelings down on paper, but he couldn't do it. I know he is following the events of the trial on a daily basis and would have preferred to be there with us.

Having filed a criminal complaint, Nathan was interviewed in September 2023 by the Children and Young Persons police unit in Meaux, Paris. His parents, sisters and friends were also contacted. His sisters remembered a boy Nathan met one summer in Mazan and invited to play in the family house. The next day, the boy's grandmother had refused to allow him to come back. What had taken place? Even the twins, although they were much younger at the time, are not without scars: they are repulsed by their bodies, fearful of men and prone to bouts of depression.

As I listen to David, I think of Céline and the rest of his family. A full enquiry had been made into Nathan's accusations. Dominique was questioned about them in

June 2024 and, as ever, denied everything. Nathan is represented by the same lawyer as Gisèle, and she is still awaiting the prosecutor's decision. If he chooses to proceed with charges, Nathan will have the chance to prepare himself for a trial. If the prosecutor declines, on the basis that there is insufficient evidence, my nephew will have to learn to live with this gaping hole, deprived of any form of closure. I understand intimately what he is facing.

David continues:

'My sister is caught up in one of the toughest fights of her life. My thoughts are with her, and I want her to know that we will always be by her side. Just as I want to say to all the other women out there: do not be afraid to denounce your predators. The rule of silence has been broken. You must speak up.

'This trial is not just about Gisèle Pelicot. It's about the destruction of an entire family.

'And yet, even though we've been crushed, my family is determined to rebuild itself. The man sitting to my left will disappear and we will write a new story for ourselves in which he has no place.'

Later, I talk to David about the reserves of power he accessed for his speech. The trial has opened his eyes to a terrible social reality. It has made him ask himself what it is to be a man, a father and a brother. It has made him look into the eyes of the accused and ask what lies in the depths of their souls. It has made him look at the crowd outside the courtroom and ask himself: *where are all the men*? Week after week, those who turned up to show their support for Gisèle were almost entirely female. Week after week, those who wrote articles and letters to express their indignation and anger were almost entirely female. Why so few men? Did they lack the necessary courage? Did they think it was not their place? Did they think it wasn't their problem? I can tell that David is dismayed by this absence, this resounding silence. Weeks later, he starts using social media to exhort other men to step up, to take a stand. All too aware of the symbolic weight of his status as both a man and Dominique's son, he feels acutely his duty to stand up for women in their fight against oppression, for victims in their fight against predators.

* * *

It's Florian's turn, our sensitive little brother. His ex-wife, Aurore, is with us in the courtroom, seated to my right. Later, she will talk publicly about the ravages of rape, abuse and incest, and how victims struggle to free themselves from their legacy of pain and suffering. As Florian walks towards the box, I know how important our presence and our focused love and attention is to him.

'In our family, we share laughter, not tears. Not once did I see my mother cry during the four months she lived with us after leaving Mazan.

'She lived in denial during those first months after everything blew up. It wasn't easy to watch. But it's easy to understand: how do you untangle yourself from 50 years of your life? How do you watch 50 years burn to the ground before your very eyes?

'We were all thrown off the edge of a cliff.

'We never saw it coming.

'How do you reinvent yourself as a son, as a father? Who has the instruction manual?

'Now we're just surviving. Nothing more.

'Our family was destroyed, and we found ourselves in Hell. What kind of foundation can we find on which to rebuild?

'Caroline's just clinging on. What she has now you can barely call a life.

'I believe Aurore. I believe Caroline. I believe Nathan. My conviction is absolute.

'I want you all to forget the name of the criminal, of the monster in this room. I want you all to remember that of the victim.'

He explains, with delicate precision, the unease he felt *before* about his place in the family. He wants to take a paternity test, to finally resolve the doubts he has about his father. He talks about the warning signs he missed, which he failed to interpret correctly. He talks about his pain, about all he too has lost. As David had done, time and again, he turns towards Dominique and recalls the values he talked about endlessly while raising him. The hypocrisy of it all leaves him stunned. He confronts Dominique, who sits hunkered down in apparent sadness but still stubbornly silent: 'Why did you do it? You always said our mother was a saint, but all the while it turns out you were the devil incarnate. You taught us that love was the one thing that really mattered. What do you know of love?'

* * *

As I watch my brothers, I feel their words buoy me up and am filled with love for them. Without them, I wouldn't be in the courtroom today. Without them, I wouldn't be able to drag myself up to testify one last time.

Finally, it's my turn. Once again, I face the court. Once again, I face that man.

I was the one who had asked that I be allowed to speak once more. I didn't just ask, I insisted, driven by the frustration I felt with the miserly amount of time I was accorded first time around. I had to overcome our lawyer's hesitations. Nobody quite understood how urgent this felt to me. I didn't simply want to do it: I had to do it.

This is what I say:

'I sat here with my brothers through the opening weeks of this trial. When I stopped coming, I found I couldn't just go back to everyday life. I knew then that the truth I sought – the truth about what happened to me – was never going to emerge. I knew when I read the report written by Doctor Paul Bensussan, which cost me so many sleepless nights before the trial opened. I knew again when I saw how the trial was going to play out.

'As far as I'm concerned, I'm the forgotten victim of this trial.

'Two photos overturned my life. I say two, but I'm sure there were more. I know my father drugged me and abused me. I know it. I just can't prove it. In 2023, I founded the organisation Don't Put Me Under for myself and all the other victims who remain unheard, who, like me, cannot point to solid and tangible evidence. Because, apparently, where there's no proof, there's no victim. Gisèle Pelicot is an exceptional case – less than one per cent of victims have access to the kinds of evidence that document the crimes she suffered. All the others are never heard, never believed. Without proof, they don't exist.

'Their fight is mine, but it hasn't come cheap. It's cost me my sleep, it's cost me my mental health, it's cost me all prospect of healing. But I won't stop fighting for the means to prevent and detect this crime. Day after day, I will hammer away until the victims of chemical submission are given the help and support that is their right.'

Like my brothers before me, I turn towards Dominique and speak to him directly:

'I know you lack the honesty, the courage, and – absurd as it seems – the love that it would take to own up to the truth about me. I know you gave in to your incestuous desires. I know you drugged me and abused me. And, because I know all this, my life has been on hold for the past four years.'

* * *

I had to confront him once again. I needed him to know that I didn't believe him, that I would never stop pursuing him, never relinquish my right to the truth, never let him fob me off, never be vanquished by his glacial indifference.

Dominique has yet to address the court. He will do so tomorrow, but I know he will stick to his lies and his silence. Just as I know that my fight for the truth will continue.

No matter how slim the chances of success, I will pursue him another day, in another court, in the hope that one day he will reveal what he has always hidden from us: the truth, the whole truth and nothing but the truth.

I feel no satisfaction as the day draws to a close. I have dinner with my brothers, Céline and Aurore. Each of us is uniquely aware what it has cost the others to speak out in court. Each of us is uniquely aware of the consequences of Dominique's acts, whose ripple effect reaches well beyond ourselves to our partners and our children. Two days later, our lawyers, Antoine Camus and Stephane Babonneau, will try as best they can to present an inventory of all we have suffered. However, in the end they admit that a full reckoning is impossible and they can only offer 'a mere sample of the profound torment inflicted upon this family by rape'.

We bid each other goodnight after this brief moment of respite. But we know our parting words ring hollow. Tomorrow Gisèle and Dominique will address the court for the last time. Tonight, none of us will know any sleep.

Tuesday, 19th November 2024

The day opens with the last of the accused attempting to explain away what happened. He echoes all who went before him – the same falsehoods, the same pathetic excuses, the same self-pity, the same refusal to confront the reality of rape: 'I failed to behave like a man … I was thinking with my penis … I lost my ability to reason.'

Then my mother is invited to address the court.

'The last of the accused has now spoken and once again I have had to listen to words that should never have been uttered. Although I knew what to expect, I have grown tired of this nauseating litany. So few have admitted to rape, so many have denied it. When, exactly, did I give my consent? When, exactly, did they say to themselves, *This is all above board, I don't have to leave*? When, exactly, did these men decide that there was no reason to call the police and recount all they had seen? Are there any excuses we have not heard? "I was manipulated. I'd been drugged. I had no idea what was going on." And they call this the Gisèle Pelicot trial. The cowardice of men – that's what's on trial here.

'One of the accused told the court he respected me. Clearly, he understands the definition of respect as well as he does the definition of rape.

'In our patriarchal society rape is dismissed as banal, commonplace, unexceptional. It's time to look at rape for what it really is.'

The defence lawyers are unleashed upon Gisèle with their niggling, heartless questions. Suddenly, one of them questions statements made by David, Florian and myself concerning the photos of me and the photoshopped images of my mother and myself. My heart stands still. I need to hear my mother stand up for me against Dominique. I need her to acknowledge the unanswered questions that have left her children in doubt and despair. I need her to recognise that all our certainties are gone, the life we all shared ground underfoot with contempt.

But she doesn't. She won't speak, other than to repeat, twice over: 'I would rather not answer that question.' I feel a pit open up beneath me. Her silence speaks volumes.

It marks a watershed. I thought we had the instinctive loyalty of a clan, that we were all in this together, united against our enemies, and, above all, against Dominique. But no. I am struck by a cold and callous truth. My mother doesn't believe me.

I had begun to sense this while first writing my book, but I had pushed it aside, preferring to believe that nothing could overcome the strength of our ties. Never have I known such pain as I experienced during those few minutes as her silence resounded throughout the courtroom and gleeful looks stole across the faces of the defence lawyers. I had spent four years doing everything I could to be there for my mother, to nurture the bond that meant so much to me. Suddenly, I was completely alone in a place of despair and nobody seemed to notice.

She had faced a similar question in the opening days of the case. When asked if she shared my conviction that my father could have drugged and sexually abused me, our two lawyers had advised her to reply 'I can't rule it out.'

That was an eternity ago. Since then, she has heard the testimony of all her children. She has heard David and Florian insisting that they believe me and begging Dominique to speak the truth – the whole truth – for once in his life. She has seen my desperate need to be freed from doubt. She knows my mental health is teetering on the edge.

But she says nothing.

It's such a slap in the face that I feel compelled to flee the courtroom. My brother David, also reeling from the blow, accompanies me. For both of us, it's the coup de grâce, after so many betrayals. Everything we've gone through over the past four years makes it impossible for me to accept her words. I recall the ten days I spent in a psychiatric facility, an experience as exhausting as it was necessary. I had fled there to sleep, to be alone with my thoughts, to seek a way to overcome all I was facing. The psychiatric staff had warned me that I would never find the healing I needed and craved, neither in the courtroom nor after the trial, and that I would have to learn to live without the mother-daughter relationship I had cherished so dearly. They didn't hesitate to call my yearning a therapeutic dead end, hoping to shock me into moving on and finding a different way to heal my wounds.

My mother and I have led different lives. We belong to different generations. We haven't lived through the same struggles. We don't share the same sources of indignation. So, of course, we react differently. In the courtroom I felt empowered to speak out, to lower my guard and go on the offensive. Her instinct was to be discreet, to choose dignity, to protect herself through her composure.

Despite all the psychiatrists had said, I had clung to a

shred of hope. I was her only daughter. She couldn't abandon me – certainly not in the arena of the courtroom. But the facts had just proven me wrong.

* * *

The defence lawyers rush into the breach opened by her refusal to answer the question. One even points out: 'Your daughter has just left the room because you seem unable to recognise that she is a victim.' Gisèle won't answer any questions about me, nor about the cold cases, nor about the rest of the family. She stakes out her position: 'The case is not about my family. I have to focus on me. The trial is about me, even if all of us are victims.' I wonder if my mother won't allow herself to believe Nathan or me – is it because she thinks it's the only way to protect herself psychologically?

I know that the defence lawyers are anything but disinterested, and that their questions are designed to destabilise our mother, to throw doubt on her judgement. A cheap, absurd shot, but the defence lawyers will try anything.

Their twisted tactics lead them to insist upon my status as a victim while Dominique pours out yet another series of lies, trying to pull everyone's strings – denying having taken any photos of me, insisting he had never seen them, and certainly never put them online, then admitting he can't really remember, then hesitating over whether they show me or another victim (despite having formally admitted beforehand that they were of me), then saying he was blackmailed into photoshopping images. It is, paradoxically, a defence lawyer who decries Dominique's unconvincing testimony: 'We can't sit and listen to such absurdities! It is inconceivable that you can't remember any of this.' And then, finally, they get to the point, hammering home Gisèle's refusal to speak as proof of her complicity with her torturer: 'When called upon to choose between Caroline and you, Mr Pelicot, you're the one she sided with.'

When our own lawyers grill Dominique about his ever-changing, ever-contradictory declarations about the two photos of me under sedation, one of them tells him: 'This is probably the last time you'll have your daughter before you, Mr Pelicot. If you stick to your current position, you're condemning her to an eternity in Hell. Are you aware how perversely cruel your position is? Do you not have it in you to offer her something better? I ask you to give her a clear, humane reply.'

Dominique answers, once again: 'I never touched my children or my grandchildren. I can't remember whether or not I took those photos. Caroline, even if you don't believe me, I never touched you.'

I know I'm not allowed to intervene. I know the presiding judge would be within his rights to cut me off and order me to leave the proceedings. But I can't think rationally. My existence is at stake. My reaction is visceral.

I yell: 'You're lying! You're lying! Your lies are all you have now. You will die alone surrounded by them. You are despicable.'

I hurl the same words at him, just as virulently, when he sadistically assures one of the defence lawyers that the person he most wants to see when sent back to prison is me. Just so that we can have, in his words, 'one last little talk'. How can he say such things? How can he keep serving up such lies? How can Gisèle, given all she knows, ask me to 'get a grip on myself' when it's my last chance to learn the truth?

Despite all the criticism of my failure to exhibit Gisèle's prudent reserve before the court, I only have one regret when I think back to these endlessly drawn-out days, each mutating from potentially decisive to appallingly painful as they fail to reveal the truth: having given rein to my anger, having cursed him time and again, I could have used a different approach with Dominique. Given his twisted personality, I could have tried to be as cynical and cunning as him, throwing myself to my knees and begging him to tell me the truth.

But, even then, would he have revealed it?

Wednesday, 20th November 2024

At the start of the trial, Dominique's lawyer, Béatrice Zavarro, told me that she would do her utmost to make him tell me the truth. She tries to keep her promise, relying on the trust built up between the two of them through the four years following his arrest. She keeps nudging him with prudent, well-chosen questions, but he doesn't budge. At one point, he offers up a rambling account of difficult moments during my youth he helped me overcome, as if these distant memories would prove once and for all that he was a good father: a surgical intervention when I was 14; an attack by a group on a bus bringing me back from school; an aggressive boyfriend a few years later; the nights he waited for me in his car during school dances. I have many memories like these – once happy, now poisoned by the lies that surrounded them.

But this was neither the time nor the place to bring them up, no matter what emotions they appeared to inspire in him.

I knew that once our lawyers presented their arguments, the court would go into recess. From then until the day the verdicts are announced, I will neither see my father nor set foot in Avignon. I feel obliged to make one last effort to reach him. He is about to leave the dock when I rush across the courtroom like a child tormented by the cruelty of the world around her. Everyone's eyes are on me. The presiding judge places his hand gently on my shoulder and asks me to remain silent, reminding me that the time has passed and I no longer have the right to speak. But I can't hold back, whispering my words to the one person who has to hear them: 'Dominique, you had two and a half months to tell me the whole truth. You owed me that. I waited for you. Two and a half months, waiting and hoping.' He begins to answer me, speaking to me as his daughter, speaking like he used to *before*, but I cut him off. I tell him it's all over. The time for a father to speak to his daughter has gone. It will never return.

* * *

I'm finally on a train going back to Paris, thinking over how powerless and unhappy I felt through these past days.

Then I recall the closing speech of one of my lawyers, Antoine Camus. He had denounced the many flaws of our legal system, saying: 'The charge sheet laid before the court acts as a constraint upon the civil party to the prosecution, fixing hard limits to what can be debated and preventing a full account of the crime.' For him, this was akin to 'a form of self-willed judicial blindness'. He gave many examples of these failings: there is no means of accurately qualifying a crime of mass rape carried out repeatedly over a period of 10 years; in penal law, there is no notion of collective responsibility; in the years since his arrest, the people behind the site coco.gg that Dominique Pelicot had used to recruit the co-accused had not yet been prosecuted; there is no means of bringing charges relating to the years of misplaced therapy my mother was forced to undergo, nor for the sexually transmitted diseases inflicted upon her.

As for the one charge relating to me – 'taking, possessing, or transmitting a sexual image without consent' – he described it as completely inadequate. I would have said neither just nor fair.

Counsellor Camus had quoted the investigating magistrate, Judge Journot, whose preparatory work determined the charges for which the accused would stand trial. She had referred to me as 'the unfinished business of this dossier', set to one side because of the constraints under which she operated and the necessity of bringing the accused to trial within a reasonable timeframe. In her report she talked of the photos of me as 'a slice of lost time', a mystery that the trial could not address.

A week later, the Director General of the École Polytechnique, Laura Chabaud, would say something similar. Recalling Dominique's constant denials concerning the photos of me, she asked: 'How on earth could you forget taking such a photo?' She expressed her compassion for the state of doubt in which I had been left concerning the horrors – her term – he could have inflicted upon me. She admitted her frustration with the judicial process 'which should never abandon a victim by the wayside. But the law requires concrete evidence. Our investigations' – partial at best, because no one had thought to ask me to undertake a toxicological analysis the day I was shown the photos – 'failed to provide an objective basis on which to base any charges.' However, she recognised the consequences for me: 'We understand her pain, whose legitimacy cannot be denied, but our legal framework is unable to accommodate all such suffering.'

These words echo constantly in my mind because the majority of victims of rape and violence in a family context have heard something similar: there are no grounds for prosecution; there is insufficient proof; there are no concrete elements; the crime is covered by a statute of limitations; the accused have been acquitted for failure to prove their crime beyond reasonable doubt; and so on, and so forth. The message is clear: your suffering is a foreign language as far as the judicial system is concerned; it will never be understood, never attain the status of truth, never be investigated, never be compensated, never be brought to a close.

Can such a situation be allowed to continue? Can we just shrug and say that nothing can be done? No. I will not accept this, not for myself, nor for all the victims out there.

The reality that neither Dominique nor the justice system have recognised my status as a victim has left me with a hollow feeling deep inside, an intolerable sense of injustice, and a constantly aching wound. We can do better. Our laws and judicial system can be changed to protect and succour all the unacknowledged victims. I intend to have new charges brought against Dominique, not just for me but for all the victims we push aside and refuse to see. Never have I felt anything with such conviction: this is my fight, and I will not give up.

Looking Forward

Now that the trial is over, the fight goes on for all the victims.

I can't say this often enough. It's the only thing I can think about.

Approximately 99 per cent of the victims of chemical sub-mission lack objective proof and are deprived of timely access to toxicological tests. I can't stop thinking of them. My situation is – appallingly – the norm.

I can't stop thinking of other, less distinct, figures too: the other victims of Dominique Pelicot. Given the scale and serial nature of his known crimes, how many did he prey upon during the 20 blank years between 1990 and his final arrests?

As one of our lawyers, Antoine Camus, put it, '[I] find it hard to believe that from 1999 to his first arrest, Dominique Pelicot whiled away his time playing Mahjong … My clients, unable to exclude any hypotheses and expecting the worst, will spend the years ahead anxiously awaiting further discoveries.'

During the trial, it was announced that Dominique Pelicot could be being charged in connection with two other crimes, despite his claims of innocence. Mr Camus agrees with us: the worst is to be expected. This is yet another reason for me to fight on for other women, other victims.

* * *

On 31st October 2022, two years after the discovery of all that Dominique Pelicot had done to my mother, I was once again plunged into a whirlpool of horror. A world of cheap, sordid crime movies.

I had spent the preceding two years compulsively paging through the dossier that recorded my father's abominable crimes – subjugating my mother with chemical submission, the constant flow of new recruits to rape her, an ever-increasing horde impossible to count. I flinched each time I faced this catalogue of atrocities, but I was trying to understand the split personality of the man who had raised me and to come to terms with all I had failed to see over an entire decade.

On that day, I was blindsided when a sickening prequel to the story we knew all too well came to light.

My brother David had called me a few days beforehand. He had learned from a high-ranking police officer in the Serious Crimes Unit in Paris that Dominique Pelicot was the subject of a new criminal investigation. Over the phone, the officer wouldn't say more than that it was a very serious crime that had taken place long before the Mazan rapes, and that the investigating team would like to question David and myself. Florian, our younger brother, was excluded because he was thought to have been too young at the time to be helpful to the enquiry.

We are asked to come to the massive police headquarters that sits in the north-western corner of the Paris. I can still recall every moment we spent there. Questions buzz around my head as we walk in. What does this new enquiry mean? What fresh atrocities await us, their claws ready to tear into the fabric of our lives? I start to armour myself, telling myself this was inevitable. Given the unprecedent crimes we knew had occurred within our family circle, there had to be others waiting to come to light.

It is early afternoon and the police officers who are waiting for us seem to be on tenterhooks. I can't help noticing that one of them is extremely pale. He watches warily and weighs each word before uttering it, knowing that what he has to say will mark us for life. He tells us he knows how much we have suffered in the context of the Mazan affair, but that he needs our help and has questions he cannot avoid asking. He warns that a second shock awaits us, no easier to absorb than the first.

'We've linked your father's DNA to a crime scene from 1999. A case of attempted rape. It wasn't our original focus, as we were working on a different cold case, an unsolved instance of rape and murder from December 1991. But when we noticed the similarities between the modus operandi in the two cases, we began to suspect your father. Now we fear that your father might have been a serial predator.'

Attempted rape. Murder. I recoil in my chair, bathed in cold sweat at the idea that there is more to come. Dominique – the man I no longer call Dad – looms balefully in my mind. I can almost hear his perverse chortle echoing in my ear from the deep, dark pit that he dug beneath us.

We're dealing with the same team that tracked notorious French serial killers Guy Georges, Michel Fourniret and François Vérove, known as Poxface due to his acne scars. They are so notorious that even I, who never took an interest in such things, have heard of them. That Dominique Pelicot might count as one of their peers is a chilling thought.

I realise that whatever scraps I can dig up from my past,

whatever answers I can give to their questions, may prove incredibly important. I may hold the secret to a whole new avenue of investigation.

As they take us upstairs and through a maze of antiseptic corridors, I feel terror rising in my throat and find it hard to breathe. I flush hot, then shiver with cold. I feel like I've been cut off from the outside world, as if I've been pushed into an underground tunnel and forced to crawl forwards, deeper into the dark.

They split us up, taking David to a room further down the corridor. We are to be questioned separately so that our answers can be compared.

'Where did you live with your parents? Where did you grow up? What were the addresses? What were the houses like?

'What jobs did your father have? Where did he go to work?

'How many cars did your father have? What makes and models?

'Can you recall any ether in a cupboard at home?

'Did you ever see any electrical cables or braided rope in any of your father's cars?

'Did he keep a toolbox in his car with screwdrivers, or cutters, or any other kind of blade?

'How did he dress when he left for work? Did he have a beige or grey overcoat?

'Would you have described your father as obsessive?'

Six hours of questions and answers. I finally ask one of my own, looking to establish some kind of context, but the officer sitting across from me tells me he cannot share any of the information they have gathered. I insist. He's mentioned a young woman that Dominique attacked in 1999. How old was she? He decides that's a detail I can have: 20 years old. There and then, I feel the darkness swirling towards me. In 1999, I was 20 and still lived with my parents. The evening in question, having assaulted and attempted to rape this young woman, he no doubt came home as usual, sat down to dinner with us, wished us all a good night and then went peaceably off to bed as if nothing had happened. Ice must have run in the veins of this man who had perfected his ability to fool us, never appearing without a mask. I knew nothing about who he really was, about his dark impulses and macabre dreams. I lived with a man who was a complete stranger to me.

Fortunately, David is there when I emerge from the interview room. I collapse into his arms, having spent hours providing the most detailed answers I could. The memories

I plundered for the investigators are strangely vivid, full of sights and smells, including the layouts of houses and the interiors of cars, and a host of tiny things. I had served up a thousand details that would normally have seemed so banal, but that now seem loaded with sinister significance.

New Horrors

I was born in January 1979, four and a half years after my brother David.

I remember every address at which the four – and then five, after Florian came along in 1986 – of us had lived. First of all, an apartment in a well-tended building surrounded by trees in a small town to the south-east of Paris. Then a house a few kilometres down the road that my father restored, which we sold a few years after the birth of Florian. Financial and marital problems then drove us into a detached house on the banks of the river Marne to the east of the capital city, provided to my mother by her employer. Here I would live until I turned 25 and met the man who would become my husband. These addresses form the backdrop to scenes from my life *before*, when the family lived happily together, even when facing tough times.

Dominique's professional life was chaotic. He had trained as an electrician but wanted to try his hand at real estate, passing from one agency to the next. There were long periods of unemployment interspersed with short-lived jobs. At one point, he became a salesman for a company that installed home security systems. He finally decided to resume work as an electrician, creating a company with an associate that installed high- and low-voltage networks for commercial and industrial clients.

During that period, he would often come home late at night, complaining of installations that had to be completed out of hours.

I can summon up each and every one of his cars: a Renault 19, a black Renault 25, a grey Fuego, a white Peugeot 205 that my mother drove, a black Smart and a white van for work. A working electrician, all of his vehicles were equipped with toolboxes, pleated cables and spools of wire. Amongst his tools, he had a particular fondness for the traditional wood-handled folding knives sold under the brand Opinel.

A large blue container full of ether sat on a shelf in the medicine cabinet in the kitchen. I had a dog, Aster, who twice gave birth to a litter of puppies. On both occasions, my father used the ether to put them to sleep before tossing them into a plastic bag and drowning them.

I recall my father's appearance back then, dapper in

his beige overcoat with his black briefcase. Except on the occasions when he wore his grey one. When he came home from work in the evening, he headed straight for a cupboard in the upstairs corridor that linked my room and David's. He couldn't rest until everything was put away in its proper place. Everything he owned was stored neatly, be it in the house, in the garage or in his car.

At the time I didn't really understand why the investigators asked me such a vast array of questions. Only later, when they started to reveal a few details, did I come to appreciate why they sought out so much information and how even the smallest of observations could prove crucial. They were searching for the pieces of a jigsaw they were privy to and I was not. It seemed crazy at the time, but later it made perfect sense.

Both cases being investigated involved young women who worked in real estate. Sophie Narme was 23 years old. In 1991, she had just begun working for a property agency in inner Paris. Marion was only 20 when she was assaulted in 1999. In both cases, they were contacted by a man who said he was interested in acquiring a property. He was only interested in top-floor apartments and wanted to visit them immediately.

Sophie Narme was killed by a man who had called her the day before and made an appointment for 10.30 a.m.

on the 4th December 1991. That morning at 8.30, Sophie left her home in a prosperous suburb to the west of Paris wearing a skirt suit cinched with a Chanel belt, glancing at her Cartier watch and proudly clutching her Vuitton handbag. Her birthday was not long past and her parents had been generous. A beautiful and elegant young woman, she had recently spent a year as an au pair in Pennsylvania. On her return, she allowed herself a few weeks in Cannes and then, helped by her father-in-law, found a job as an estate agent in Paris.

Her destination was rue Manin in the 19th arrondissement, where she found a parking space in front of the building where she was showing the apartment. Her client was probably right on time. They walked through the entrance hall, across the courtyard and into a second building hidden from the street. There was no lift, so they walked up the six flights of stairs.

Almost all the neighbours were out, either at work or doing their shopping. Only one recalls the noise of feet going up the stairs. Sophie must have used a key to open the apartment on the sixth floor, because the police later determined that the door had not been forced. In they went, and for a while Sophie may have believed that it was just another viewing with an interested client.

Without anyone hearing a sound, not even the neighbour in the apartment underneath, Sophie was violently attacked, rendered unconscious with ether, raped and strangled.

At 9.30 p.m., her employer came to the apartment, anxious at having heard nothing from her all day and after she had missed several appointments. He was the one who found her body.

The police noticed the smell of ether straight away. They noted that the victim lay on her stomach, arms twisted behind her back, her left cheek pressed hard against the floor, her face hidden by her hair. She had been tied up at some point and then released.

She was half naked. When turned over, her face showed extensive bruising around her mouth, her left brow, her right eye, her right cheek and her lower lip. Her bra had been ripped open to expose her breasts.

Aside from the blows to her face, she had many puncture wounds and a wide cut under her left breast. The condition of her nails indicated that she had used them to lash out, trying to defend herself. Her murderer had pulled down her tights and underwear, leaving them bunched around her ankles. As for her high heels, they had been meticulously posed alongside her body – a detail that haunted all those who visited the crime scene or worked on the case thereafter.

The room had been turned upside down, a mute witness to the violence Sophie had suffered and the force with which she had fought back. She had been wearing several rings, and every single one had come off in the struggle. Some were twisted, others broken.

Her killer had to bind her up and put her under to overcome her forceful resistance. Having raped her, he used her Chanel belt to strangle her.

Her handbag had been emptied onto the floor before being placed neatly alongside a wall.

Her aggressor must have carried away several objects from the scene of the crime. The next day, Sophie's mother pointed out all the missing items of jewellery: a Santos watch by Cartier with an octagonal face in gold and steel; a gold bracelet with large links and a double safety catch; a necklace of woven gold; a gold pendant in the form of the Pink Panther; a wide golden ring with a single diamond; a narrow golden ring with a blue sapphire.

Sophie's Vuitton wallet and chequebook holder were missing, along with a wad of cheques from the Meulan branch of the Société Génerale bank. Her passport and her Société Générale credit card, not due to expire until 1992, were also gone.

Sophie had been lured into the apartment to be raped and killed.

Her killer's sperm was found in Sophie's vagina during an autopsy carried out on the night of the 4th December 1991, but this crucial evidence was subsequently mishandled and lost.

On the 11th May 1999, Marion, 20 years old, sees a man looking at her through the window of the estate agency where she is a trainee. He comes in and says he is urgently looking for an apartment to buy and would like to visit any they might have available that very day. Marion takes him at his word and shows him a number of listings, one of which is a duplex apartment for which she has the keys. He agrees to see it, and she offers to take him in her own car. Before he gets in, he nips off to collect a few items from his own, parked nearby.

When they reach their destination, Marion leads him into the apartment and puts her handbag and car keys on the worktop of the open plan kitchen downstairs. The man quizzes her about the property and seems enthusiastic about it, putting Marion at ease. They go up the apartment's inner staircase to look at the two bedrooms under the eaves, along with a dressing room and a bathroom.

As he looks at one of the bedrooms, the man wonders

aloud whether his furniture would fit in. He asks Marion if she can check the dimensions of the room. Seeing this as another encouraging sign, she nips back downstairs to get a tape measure from her handbag and returns to the room. As the room has a sloping ceiling, she has to bend over to measure the height of one of the walls. As she does so the man comes up behind her, immobilising her against the wall and wrapping his left arm around her neck.

Convinced of his intention to strangle her, she tries to wriggle free but cannot break his grip.

He orders her to lie down on the floor. She drops towards the ground and manages to break away from him. The only way out is down the staircase. Twice she manages to evade his grasp and sprint towards it. Twice he catches up with her and tosses her violently across the room. Her escape route cut off, she contemplates her death at the hands of her aggressor.

But she continues to struggle, lashing out as he pounds her face. He manages to push her down, stomach first, onto the floor. She becomes aware of a strange, intoxicating smell as he covers her mouth and nose with a piece of cloth. She begins to choke and to lose sensation. Her limbs become heavy and distant. They cease to respond to her orders to fight. She feels her very being dissolve. Something chemical has stolen her will. He now has complete control over her.

He ties her wrists behind her back and pulls her trousers down. She still has her underwear on, but he is grabbing it and she has no doubt about what will happen next.

Bound and gagged, bruised and stripped, woozy with ether, Marion goes limp. With no means to defend herself, convinced her last moment has come, she barely has the strength to breathe. But her survival instincts haven't left her. Lying on her back, she pretends to have fallen asleep, but she keeps flexing her hands and wrists, loosening the cords that bind them. Although she still feels detached from her body, she can sense her attacker's every move. The man tugs her trousers off completely and then removes his own, carefully folding them up before setting them aside. He starts to pull her underwear down her thighs. Conscious that there are mere seconds left before he will rape her, she fights her way back into her own body and throws it forward, ramming her head into his. He hits back, castigating her as he does so, but she lashes out too. As he attempts to strangle her once again, she grabs his testicles and tugs at them violently, sending him staggering back. He falls to his knees, casting around for something on the floor. She gets to her feet, stumbles away and somehow makes it to a nearby cupboard. She throws herself inside. As she pulls the door closed, her hand discovers there's a bolt allowing it to be locked from the inside. She rams it shut.

For an excruciating length of time, she can hear him moving about, walking around the apartment, using the toilets. Finally, silence descends.

After four hours in the darkness, she slides back the bolt. She can't bear to wait any longer, and is ready to face death if her aggressor is still there, waiting for her.

She isn't alone for long. Her employer turns up, worried by her long absence. He discovers her shaking with fear, covered in bruises, her legs bare, her feet naked. He gathers her up and rushes her to the nearest police station.

Traces of blood are found on Marion's shoes and on the carpet of the apartment. It isn't hers. A DNA test undertaken 23 years after the attempted rape reveals that it's Dominique's. In February 2024, he and Marion are brought face-to-face by the investigating magistrate in charge of this cold case. She formally identifies him as her aggressor.

For the first 48 hours of his detention, Dominique denies any connection to the attack on Marion. When told of the DNA match, he changes his tune. He admits attempted rape but insists no violence was involved. He denies that he was armed in any way. When the magistrate questions him in Marion's presence, he serves up a mess of contradictions and hollow explanations, foreshadowing his testimony in the Mazan trial.

He says the desire to rape her struck him out of the blue when he glimpsed her through the window of the estate agents. A bit later, he says it came to him after they had chatted for a while at her desk. He insists that he only tied her up 'so that he could do something to her without hurting her'. He says his only goal was 'to prevent her suffering in any way'. He indicates that he bound her wrists behind her back with electrical cable, pulled so tightly it bit into her skin, only 'to avoid all the unpleasantness that later occurred when the ether didn't do its job'. He dismisses her account of the struggle, saying that at most he may have pushed her around a little. He admits to having threatened her with his car keys but not with a blade of any kind. He says she head-butted him but otherwise did him no harm and denies ever having hit her.

Not so, according to the A&E doctor who examined Marion right after the assault. Her medical records showed subcutaneous bleeding on her forehead, dark bruising across the arc of her eyebrows and on her left shoulder, torn skin and deep scratches on her throat, and the telltale bruises of strangulation. Dominique claims he was the one who brought the struggle to an end, announcing: 'That's enough, I'm going.' Yet another shameless confection of lies.

As for the rape and murder of Sophie Narme, he denies any connection. Because all the samples taken from the victim and the crime scene were lost, it's impossible to do a DNA test. He knows this.

But the modus operandi for Sophie was startlingly similar: the ether, the restraints, the menacing blade, the age and profession of the victim, and the way both the women's clothes were wrenched off. All of this, in addition to the geographical proximity of the two attacks, cause alarm bells to start ringing in the ears of the investigators from the cold case team, who are used to reconstructing the trajectory of serial offenders.

Everything I know about Sophie and Marion I learned later, long after the hours spent being quizzed by the cold case team. I've become obsessed with the two cases. They keep me up at night. I want to know all that Dominique has done – how long he has been preying upon women, when he first gave way to his impulses, how many victims he has left in his wake. There is not a doubt in my mind that his list of crimes goes way beyond what we currently know. I am determined to see him punished for all his acts. Not a day goes by without me thinking about the victims of the man who fathered me – those whose identity is known and those whose names are yet to be discovered. My aim has never changed; the truth has to be revealed.

In January 2023, a friend who is a journalist puts me in contact with a lawyer, Florence Rault, who represents the families of Marion and Sophie Narme. For over 20 years, she has worked tirelessly on their behalf. I need to learn all she knows, to immerse myself in these two intimately connected cases. I can learn all the steps she had to take to unearth the reality of the crimes, the individual identities and personalities of each victim, and all the obstacles she had to overcome. She is willing to meet me, and we do so several times.

Sophie Narme's mother hired Florence Rault in 2000, after nine years of waiting for progress to be made in her daughter's case. When Florence Rault recovered the dossier, she found several mistakes and procedural errors. Some of the objects and samples taken from the crime scene had never been examined and others had been glossed over, barely considered. The most serious mistake was that the sperm recovered during the autopsy had been either contaminated or lost when shipped to a laboratory for analysis. Florence Rault had tried her utmost, 13 years later, to interview the pathologist, the transporter and the lab crew, but all her requests were denied on the grounds that too much time had gone by for anyone to remember anything useful about the incident. Outraged, she filed a case denouncing the failings of the judicial system in the case and demanding compensation. She won.

The investigating magistrate who first handled the case had put a lot of work into it. But the dossier passed from his hands to others and entered a judicial limbo. 'We haven't found a guilty party and there are no avenues left to explore.' The magistrates who inherited the case took the easy way out: case closed for lack of evidence. Florence Rault never gave up. She identified known serial rapists and offenders whose crimes appeared similar and asked that the police to pinpoint their location and activity at the time of the crime. Single-handedly, she ensured that the case was never closed. The cold case specialists answered her call, and they worked tirelessly to retrieve whatever information and evidence they could from the original files. Had the case been closed, no connection would ever have been made between Marion and Sophie Narme. If it were not for this one lawyer's efforts, the full extent of Dominique's criminal past would have remained hidden, tucked away in society's blind spot.

Joining the Dots

In 2022, Florence Rault receives a call from Nathalie Turquey, the magistrate heading up the cold case team for the Paris region. She is informed that the case of Sophie Narme, on which she has been working for 22 years, has been merged with another. This is when she first hears of Marion's case, closed long before due to the French statute of limitations. It's Dominique's blood, found on Marion's shoe, that puts the case back on the radar. Everyone assumes that the blood was the result of a blow from Marion, but later Dominique insists that he had accidentally torn the skin around one of his fingernails that day, downplaying the assault on his victim. The photos of the crime scene show blood spattered all over Marion's shoe and the carpet of the apartment. Marion thinks she struck out with a knife that Dominique had brought with him – something he stubbornly denies. All that blood from a cut or a ripped cuticle? As ever, it's the details that rip apart the web of lies.

As Florence Rault tells me about the DNA tests that were done 23 years after Dominique's attack on Marion, I realise that a major failure must have taken place within the judicial system. Dominique had been arrested in 2010, caught filming up the skirts of women shopping in a supermarket in Collégien, a town to the south-east of Paris. He had been made to undergo a DNA swab, but the resulting lab analysis – which should have linked him to the attempted rape of Marion – was lost in the system. The horrors of the next ten years could have been prevented. We would not have had to wait until 2020 and his arrest for similar behaviour for his heinous crimes to be discovered.

If the system were less dysfunctional – if everybody had the competence and commitment of Florence Rault, the first investigating magistrate to handle Marion's dossier, and the cold case team – how many more crimes would be solved? Or, for that matter, prevented.

When brought in to confront Dominique, Marion found herself in a state of panic. She trembled, found it hard to articulate her words, and felt like her brain had seized up.

Dominique was completely at ease, even allowing himself to be haughty with the investigating magistrate. To this day, Marion still has a scar on her face from the assault, not to mention the other scars deep within her psyche. When asked whether she had thought she would die on the day she was attacked, her answer was clear: 'Yes'.

Dominique was in prison in Marseille at the time of his questioning and had been brought to Paris by plane for the day. As ever, his approach to the interview was to dodge and weave. He denied that he was at the crime scene, only to retract his denial when he was told about the DNA test. He explained that he just wanted to get to know Marion and had never considered raping her. He asserted that the ether was actually proof of his good intentions, since he had just wanted to make sure she didn't feel any pain. He insists he tied her up for the same reason – to ensure she didn't come to any harm. Who could believe he was the kind of man who would seek to reduce someone to a helpless rag doll? Who indeed.

The transcript of this confrontation leaves my head spinning. It's Mazan all over again – the same attitude, the same words, both his and those of the other accused. He didn't want to rape her; he didn't think he was raping her; he never intended any harm; it was all just a big mistake. Every time he is caught, Dominique Pelicot presents himself as a man who has chosen to come clean and cooperate, whereas he never admits anything until hard proof of his guilt has been presented. All he has are his compulsive lies and his inability to keep his story straight.

During the exchange, Florence Rault is struck by Dominique's aloof indifference. He remains calm, taking his time to find his words, and always coming up with an answer, even if it differs in some significant way from an earlier one. He weighs up every question he is asked, searching for a gap he might squirm through. Marion's lawyer is convinced she is dealing with someone executing a well-practised protocol, his unnatural calm a symptom of his machine-like personality. Going through the transcript later, she has no doubt that her client was just one of many victims, that he had spent decades perfecting his predatory techniques, and that if Marion had not fought back, she would no longer be alive.

Dominique's vocabulary, in and of itself, sets alarm bells ringing for Florence Rault. When she asks him what he was doing in the street outside the estate agency on May 11th 1999, he replies he was 'out hunting', which he then explains by saying he was seeking potential prospects for the video surveillance company that then employed him. *Out hunting*. When she points out that being in possession of ether and rope suggests premeditated rape, he denies it, saying: '*On that occasion*, I brought nothing, I took no precautions, *I didn't even have gloves*.' Given that the belt used to strangle Sophie Narme showed no traces of prints or DNA, how could they avoid the conclusion that on other occasions he had indeed remembered to take his gloves?

Florence Rault's account of her encounter with Dominique Pelicot reveals something else that leaves me furious.

The meeting is cut short because Dominique has to be taken back to his prison cell in Marseille. There isn't enough time for the lawyers to ask all their questions, even after the police officers escorting him agreed to push their flight back to a later time that evening. Florence Rault formally requests an additional meeting, arguing that another face-to-face interrogation is absolutely necessary, but she is told it won't be possible – Dominique cannot be brought back to Paris a second time, and the investigating magistrate doesn't have the availability to travel to Marseille along with the two parties' lawyers. All that she obtains is a videoconference 20 days later. Predictably, with the participants hiding behind their screens, without the focus and tension of an in-person encounter, it proves completely pointless.

Florence Rault's frustration brought back an infuriating memory: her presence, as a lawyer for one of his victims, at the trial of Guy Georges, a serial killer who terrorised the east of Paris over a 20-year period. Ten days into his trial, Florence Rault was in the midst of cross-examining Guy Georges when he finally began to open up. Having offered up nothing but callous indifference since his arrest, he suddenly seemed to switch identities, revealing the child he had once been, abandoned at birth by his mother. The entire courtroom was on tenterhooks, convinced that the trial was on the verge of a breakthrough, when the presiding judge cut everything short and announced it was time for lunch. The Guy Georges who came back to the dock that afternoon was once again the stone-cold serial killer; the vulnerable child within him that the court had briefly glimpsed was never seen again.

When she had been sitting across from Dominique in the investigating magistrate's office, crafting her questions with care and scrutinising his reactions, Florence Rault believed that – having noted hesitations and contradictions, hints at cracks in his mask – his hidden, inner self was nearing the surface. Had she had more time, she might have been able to zero in on these tiny breaches in his defence, provoking him into saying more, and maybe, just maybe, bringing him face to face with his deeds and forcing him to recognise them. But no such time was given. The police and judicial system have their own unforgiving rhythms, a tightly constrained calendar, inflexible machinery, and peculiar preoccupations, none of which take into account the victims it is meant to serve.

It's not that nobody cares. The problem is systemic, born of the unwieldy, bureaucratic nature of the justice system and its obsession with cost. It has become a mechanism focused on its own constraints and priorities and increasingly disconnected from the fundamental imperative of establishing the truth.

The clock-watching that undermined Marion's case returns to haunt the trial at Mazan. One of the judges cuts off a lawyer on the grounds that 'if we carry on like this, we'll still be here next Easter' (the trial was scheduled to end before Christmas). Questions that Dominique Pelicot and his co-accused should have faced go unasked. The four months accorded to the trial – presented at the outset as an exceptional investment of time – in the end prove all too short, forcing witnesses, experts, lawyers and the civil parties to continuously hurry along, missing crucial details.

I'm not alone in thinking that the proceedings should have been allowed an extra two, if not four, months. But time is money, and the time given was doled out with a miserly hand. The Ministry of Justice can identify any trial as an 'extraordinary undertaking', triggering extra resources to allow a regional courtroom or local jurisdiction to handle a particularly complex or high-profile case. Astonishingly, this label was initially refused to the Mazan trial. Squeezed into a cramped courtroom with time allocated sparingly for each intervention, the whole thing left the impression of a rush job, with testimony cut short, subjects left unexplored, and lives skimmed over. I dread to think what the day-to-day reality is inside courtrooms dealing with trials that attract no external attention whatsoever.

Once you add up the procedural errors, the lost dossiers, the misplaced evidence, the forensic results that are never looked at, and the computer systems that fail to work, injustice seems inevitable. Add in the repetitive flaws that mar trials for rape and serious sexual offences – the same omissions, the same inappropriate choices – and things look even worse. It's not just the punishment that should fit the crime, but the process too. If you fail at that, you fail all the victims.

The Implications

The cold case team call my mother two weeks after they have spoken to me and my brother. When I next visit her, I can tell she's in denial, just as she was when the photos taken of me first came to light. She struggles to admit the things she wants to believe are impossible. 'Dominique can't have done that. There must be a mistake.' Perhaps. Perhaps she didn't live for years with a monster and a rapist. Perhaps monsters have principles and never stoop to raping or killing young women.

I am convinced Dominique is a serial rapist, and that he targeted young women who were, at the time, the same age as his daughter. Of course he denies it, and benefits from the presumption of innocence, but not for one moment do I believe that Sophie and Marion were his only victims.

The deeper I dig, the more potential cases come to light. There was an attack that took place a few weeks before the murder of Sophie Narme: Monique S., another estate agent, was showing a top-floor apartment to a man when he assaulted her; she managed to push him away and later described to police a figure that had a particular resemblance to Dominique at that point in his life. There was an attack in 2003 in a commercial building in Chelles, just across the river Marne from the house we occupied at the time, where exactly the same modus operandi was used.

Just how many women did he threaten, assault and rape? Besides my campaign to highlight the problem of chemical submission, I now work alongside those journalists, lawyers, detectives and organisations fighting to bring justice to all victims of sexual violence. Since 2020, I've been trying to establish the truth about what was done to me by Dominique. I want all the women who make up the massed ranks of forgotten victims to have the same opportunity.

Almost all the experts I have spoken with about Dominique's criminal trajectory share my conviction. My mother underwent indescribable suffering in Mazan and could so easily have been killed in the process. What I have learned since then has simply confirmed my belief that there is a vast, deadly, evil wood that we cannot see for that one tragic tree.

The discovery of these other crimes is as hard for me to process as the original shock I suffered in 2020. It destroys any lingering notion that there may ever have been a good father, a model husband, a man dedicated to his family's happiness. That there was ever anything other than a baseless imposter. Highly strung, often violent, financially irresponsible, his one talent was his ability to hide his crimes, his one source of good fortune the failings of the police and criminal justice system. There were many mistakes made by others in the system that left him free to commit more terrible acts. A compulsive liar, he organised his entire life to ensure that we never doubted anything and never questioned him. That was his one success. There were many things I should have seen but failed to.

I will never call him Dad again. I broke that bond years ago. But it has gone further: revulsion now takes the place of rejection. It's not easy to shrug off all traces of one's own father or disown the past of an entire family. But however long it takes, I don't have a choice. I have to admit that the crimes of Mazan could be extension of those that preceded them. He began raping women rendered unconscious long before age led him to seek a target closer to hand, repeating the pattern with his own wife and within the walls of his own house.

When the Mazan trial began, my suspicion of his previous crimes coloured my view of Dominique in the dock. It sickened me to see him take centre stage and play the role he had chosen for himself: a finger-wagging pedant confessing his guilt and self-righteously condemning the crimes of his fellow accused; a contrite old man asking for forgiveness for all the harm he'd done, admitting that his fantasies had led him astray, implying that age alone had tripped him up, stumbling from an exemplary life into one of crime. The falseness of it all is so apparent to me that I cannot bear the thought that others might be fooled into believing him.

The cold cases were brought up during the trial. The transcript of the confrontation of Dominique and Marion was read out in court. Hearing it read aloud, I was horrified to realise that Dominique compared Marion to me. 'I realised that she was just like my daughter.' 'Just as I pulled off her trousers, I thought to myself – she could be my daughter. That's why I stopped in my tracks. That's why I left.'

Perhaps he really did think about me. But we know that such a thought didn't stop him in his tracks. What does that reveal about his true thoughts and feelings towards me, given that if Marion hadn't fought him off and sought refuge in a cupboard, she would have been violently raped?

* * *

In the middle of the trial, *Paris Match* published a long article on the cold cases drawing a parallel between Dominique's criminal career and that of the serial killer known as Poxface. Although I was irritated by the fact that the article featured a series of family photos, its argument draws me in: '[Pelicot and Poxface] may have shared more than just sexually deviant and violent impulses – the profiles of their victims, the settings chosen for their crimes, and the modus operandi that each rigorously followed are strikingly similar.' The article's conclusion is troubling: 'Could Poxface's crimes have served as a smokescreen for the monster of Mazan, allowing him to escape justice for three decades?'

As I read, I become more and more apprehensive that still more victims are about to come to light. A name comes up I haven't heard before: Edith Martinet's naked body was found in her studio apartment in the northern suburbs of Paris on the 3rd April 1987; she had been stabbed and strangled. It has always been assumed she was one of Poxface's victims, but what if the true perpetrator was Dominique Pelicot? The final words of the article are: 'Dominique Pelicot dropped completely off the radar between the assault he committed in 1999 and the first known rapes of his wife Gisèle in 2011. What really happened during those 12 years? It seems highly unlikely that the monster of Mazan miraculously overcame his predatory instincts during that time. As far as other crimes are concerned, he of course remains innocent until proven guilty, but the justice system is now obliged to probe the dark abyss of these missing years.'

The repeated references to Dominique as a 'monster' leave me unimpressed. The term has been trotted out so many times on so many occasions it barely means anything anymore. Few realise that Dominique's true monstrosity lies in his ability to shapeshift and appear like a harmless pensioner, a reliable father and an indulgent grandfather.

* * *

I have lost so much. The foundations on which I had built my life have been left in ruins. I've lost count of the sleepless nights and the torrents of tears that Dominique, with his violence and his lies, has cost me. Less a man than a plague, he has reduced my inner life to a ravaged, sterile no man's land. But he remains my focus, and I am determined not to leave the task of revealing all the harm he has done to others, or to chance.

It's up to me to shine a spotlight on the many years when he hid his crimes behind a false identity. It's up to me to stand up for all the women who have been preyed upon, all the victims of chemical submission. That's the reason I agreed to dive deep into my memories for the cold case team. That's why I spent long hours listening to Florence

Rault dissect the assaults on Sophie Narme and Marion. That's why I want images of Dominique from the period pre-Mazan to be distributed as widely as possible, to help others put a name to the phantom that haunts them.

* * *

The Mazan trial is just the beginning. I have filed a new criminal complaint in the hope of convincing the judicial authorities to reopen the case concerning what took place in my bedroom while I was out cold. Florence Rault has agreed to take over the dossier and argue a case that will force Dominique back into the dock. It may seem that it's just my word against his but, actually, it's his words against him, too. Time and again, he compared me to my mother and to Marion. When asked by one of the lawyers why he hadn't taken any photos of his sons he answered: 'I'm not sexually interested in men.' Doesn't that mean he was sexually interested in me? Doesn't that mean incest was on his mind when he posed my unconscious body and framed me with his camera?

The chances of success of a new case are hard to determine. I will forge ahead nonetheless. I have no intention of laying down my arms.

The Fight

Antoine Camus, our lawyer, provided the court with an apt summary of what we – Gisèle, her children, her friends – lived through after discovering the chemical submission she had endured and the rapes it engendered: 'The initial reaction was disbelief. Not only had none of them, not even Gisèle, known how to read the warning signs, they hadn't even noticed their existence, and yet the signs were clearly present. The explanation is simple: nobody can imagine what is unimaginable. Caroline has grasped this essential truth. She has made it her crusade by creating an organisation that has rendered the warning signs visible and comprehensible. An authority in its field, it has been a catalyst for an ever-growing number of criminal complaints and victim statements.'

This is indeed what I sought to achieve after the Mazan affair opened my eyes to a phenomenon both intolerable and banal, an everyday occurrence claiming vast numbers of victims. Today, Don't Put Me Under can indeed claim to authoritative status, but it took a long, determined struggle to get there.

When I first started writing this book, I sought out the advice and wisdom of the heroic pioneers of the fight against sexual and domestic violence.

The first person I talked to was Doctor Ghada Hatem-Gantzer, founder of numerous support centres for victims of abuse. Ghada explains how important it is to develop a network of personalities and sponsors to create visibility, convince stakeholders of the gravity of the problem and raise funds. My own experience had taught me that domestic violence has a systemic effect, rippling out from its primary victim to the people around them. Given the abandonment and isolation I had felt, and the difficulties my mother had encountered with the medical establishment, I knew the importance of effective psychological, social and medical support, and how rare it was.

During our first encounter I realise that it was her front-line experience as a female doctor and gynaecologist that had driven her to establish the first Women's Centre. Now there are many, but she is still working hard, juggling two major projects: one involves adding a 400-square-metre extension to create a warm, welcoming space within the original Women's Centre; the other seeks to create a shelter and daycare centre for young female victims of sexual violence aged 18 to 25. At the time I was working for a well-known Swedish furniture company, and I managed to convince its directors to finance all the fixtures and fittings required by these two projects.

It's a first step for me, but I refuse to stop there.

I want to meet women who inspire me. I want to make a difference, to get involved in initiatives that have a lasting impact. Months of reflection and discussion have nourished what I believe is a unique perspective: I am convinced that the existing programmes and organisations targeting sexual and domestic violence have a blind spot when it comes to chemical submission. I talk about it with Ghada and many others working in the field. Before I throw myself into the fray, I am determined to evaluate the true scope and impact of what I instinctively believe is a huge social problem. I am ready to do my homework.

I ask for a second meeting with Ghada and ask her if she will lend her name to a campaign I hope to launch against chemical submission. I also turn to Arielle Schwab, a good friend of mine and second-in-command of a legendary advertising agency, Havas Paris. Arielle had stood by me from the moment disaster struck my family, proving herself scrupulously attentive, psychologically perceptive and intellectually astute as she helped me understand and navigate a brutal new world. Throughout her career in communications, she has lent her skills to those trying to make the world a better place, particularly when it comes to improving the lives of women. I knew I had to bring her on board, and she proved unique in her ability to understand exactly what I wanted to achieve. She didn't hesitate to join me, providing wise advice without ever dampening my enthusiasm.

Having grasped the importance of the awareness campaign I want to launch, Arielle introduces me to her talented staff, two of whom, Jeanne and Sophie, will play a crucial role. We throw ourselves into a hectic schedule, filled with brainstorming sessions, calls and meetings with third parties. Chemical submission, a type of violence cloaked in invisibility, deprives its victims of all agency: aside from inhaling and exhaling, they are absent, unconscious throughout the abuse they suffer. After months of work and constant to-ing and fro-ing, Arielle's team suggest a name for the movement I want to launch: Don't Put Me Under: End Chemical Submission. It is spot on, summing up a victim's physical and psychological trauma: don't betray me by using use drugs to sedate me.

We come up with an idea for our campaign focused on information and prevention. We want to make a short film but soon realise it would cost too much to produce and distribute widely.

Although in 2022 the first publication in France of *I'll Never Call Him Dad Again* creates an upswell of interest, few people grasp the message I try to hammer home in every interview: I'm not out to sensationalise a crime but instead want to denounce a widespread practice that represents a massive public health problem. I'm given a polite hearing by professionals, organisations and personalities. They express their shock and sympathy at the crimes my family has endured, but they appear unconvinced that anything more is called for.

During the course of my research and writing, I had spoken with Samira Djezzer, a doctor working for the National Agency for the Security of Pharmaceutical Products. I decide to call her back and ask for her help. She puts me in touch with one of her colleagues, Doctor Leila Chaouachi, an expert in chemical submission who monitors the use and abuse of pharmaceuticals in the Paris region, producing an annual report on the subject.

I will never forget my first contact with Leila. I ring her from the car park of a supermarket in Gif-sur-Yvette at a point in time when I desperately needed someone to listen to me, to show that they understood what I was going through and its effect on me. My phone call isn't a casual enquiry but a cry for help at a critical moment. I ask for her frank opinion. I fear she will think I'm simply delusional and mistaken in my belief that chemical submission is indeed an urgent problem rather than an isolated incident that afflicted my family. Her response both reassures me and at the same time breaks my heart. After all, whilst it might have been hard for me to hear that this was simply a problem particular to my family, it would have been far better for our world if I had been wrong. Leila tells me I am not mistaken, that chemical submission is a form of violence deeply rooted in many families and society at large. She speaks of its insidious and destructive nature and of the extent to which its presence is vastly underestimated, a form of institutional blindness the effect of which is catastrophic.

Leila Chaouachi fills me in on the backstory of the medical establishment's slow recognition of the scale of the problem, with the National Agency for the Security of Pharmaceutical Products finally undertaking a sweeping national enquiry in 2003. The resulting report was a first attempt to estimate the number of cases, describe the contexts in which they occurred, list the chemical substances employed and detail the consequences for the victims. Leila and her team did what they could to raise awareness, but they felt as if they were preaching to a scattered, disparate audience, if not a complete void.

A law was finally introduced in 2018 categorising chemical submission as an aggravating factor in rape. In 2021, the rise of hashtags #CallOutTheBars and #MeTooGHB, used to denounce date rape, finally gave victims a voice. As more and more are heard, the criminal use of pharmaceuticals becomes common knowledge and Drug Crisis hotlines are flooded with calls from women unwittingly exposed to psychoactive compounds, not just in bars and night clubs but also within the domestic sphere. Leila, as coordinator of an annual survey compiling the criminal complaints received by the police and the calls to hotlines for help or advice, catalogues the substances used by predators: anxiolytics, sleeping pills and allergy treatments. She details the profiles of victims, calculates the relative frequence of occasional and systematic abuse, and estimates the vast number of crimes concealed by the low percentage of victims who register a criminal complaint.

Leila agrees to come onboard. With her expertise, we can finally have an impact on public policy. Having spent years working in isolation, identifying the telltale signs of each substance, helping victims understand what has been done to them and seek justice, and elaborating strategies to prevent abuse, she provides knowledge and practical solutions we can scale-up nationwide.

Arielle, Jeanne, Sophie, Leila and I come together to craft an awareness campaign. Two photographers recruited from amongst our friends, Géraldine Aresteanu and Patrick Gaillardin, offer their services. We print out a custom T-shirt and ask 30 public figures to be photographed wearing it. Patrick builds us a website.

A year after the publication of my book, we launch a publicity blitz, hoping to spark a national conversation about chemical submission. A number of journalists prove sympathetic. One in particular, Louise Colcombet, turns in a remarkable front-page article published in the *Parisien* on 23rd May 2023. Suddenly, we're news.

We launch a public petition entitled 'Don't leave the victims of chemical submission at the bottom of a black hole'. Arnaud Gallais, co-founder of a prominent movement called Prevent and Protect, focused on violence against women and children, joins with Arielle, Leila, Ghada and me in demanding that the public authorities recognise and respond to the crisis, given that chemical submission is 'poorly identified, poorly understood, and poorly handled'. We target three government ministers: Gérald Darminin, the Interior Minister, Eric Dupond-Moretti, the Minister for Justice, and François Braun, the Health Minister, who invites me to meet him a few days later.

Our petition lays out the facts in stark fashion: most victims don't know that they are victims, given their chemically induced memory loss, the lack of clues visible to them or their immediate circle, the common diagnostic errors made by the medical profession, and the technical complexity and crushing expense of securing evidence of the crime. We demand 'a comprehensive nationwide campaign to train and inform medical professionals and the creation of an interministerial working group to pull together all the bodies necessary to tackle the problem.'

We cannot succeed without capturing the attention of and securing support from the political, governmental and administrative establishment. It alone has the means and the authority to conduct sweeping informational campaigns, train entire professions and forge new laws.

Through an unexpected back door, we find a way into the heart of the establishment. This comes to us by way of a victim of chemical submission who – unusually, but crucially – is anything but anonymous. Her name is Sandrine Josso, a sitting member of the National Assembly, the elected deputy for the Loire-Atlantique region. On the 14th November 2023, I watch her being interviewed on television. She tells how another member of the legislative branch, a senator named Joël Guerriau, drugged her – accidentally, according to him – and how she fled from his clutches, dragging herself into a taxi and insisting that she be taken straight to hospital to undergo tests to identify the substances used against her. That she has the courage and determination not only to file a criminal complaint but also name names in a live interview makes me realise that our time has come. The fight against chemical submission has just gone from a skirmish to all-out war.

Thanks to Sandrine, chemical submission is suddenly a subject of political debate. I feel compelled to join forces with her, unaware that I am about to forge a lasting friendship and that her experience will complete and confirm mine, and vice versa.

It was the immediacy of Sandrine's reaction that made her case so compelling: she grasped what was happening to her, she knew how to react, she sought out immediate medical care and analysis, and she went public without hesitation.

She realised she'd been drugged when she spotted her aggressor slip a sachet back into a drawer in his kitchen. As she stumbled from the apartment, he pursued her, joining her in the lift and followed her in the street until she managed to clamber into a passing taxi. She asked to be taken to the National Assembly, where a friend, who never questioned her account of the evening, called an ambulance to ensure that forensic evidence of the attempted chemical submission could be collected. She was taken to the Lariboisière hospital in the centre of Paris where the doctors, having ensured her condition was stable, took blood and urine samples.

Since the assault involved another elected politician, Sandrine consulted the Leader of the National Assembly, who encouraged her to register a criminal complaint. Having gone straight to a police station, she was taken in hand by a pair of empathetic female officers who offered a safe space for her to recover, recount all she had undergone and answer their questions. They provided her with the contact details of a psychologist and, losing no time, immediately ordered a search of the senator's home. Sandrine was then taken to a police lab to have hair samples taken. The senator was taken into custody and Sandrine was told she would be brought in to confront him. She retained a lawyer who explained the procedure and helped her prepare a public statement. Thanks to the police recommendation that she see a psychologist, she was able to start working on her personal journey to recovery alongside her public fight for justice.

Sandrine's experience after the assault was, in many ways, exemplary. But it was also, undoubtedly, atypical. The vast majority of victims benefit from little or none of the guidance, sympathy and investigative rigour she received.

My experience is the norm for most victims of chemical submission – years spent unaware of what happened to them, and then being perpetually denied recognition as victims. Sandrine's ordeal, which no one could doubt, made her an ideal champion for our cause.

I met her through a friend, the journalist Bruce Toussaint, who had been one of the first to interview her and provide a public forum for her story. Our first encounter left its mark on both of us. Sandrine knew little or nothing about chemical submission, since the doctors at the Lariboisière hospital had talked of it in only the most general terms when treating her. She had so many questions: what studies had been carried out, who were the experts, who were my organisation's allies, what were our priorities and what could she do to help?

I invited her to become a figurehead and spokesperson for Don't Put Me Under. She immediately accepted and began working regularly with Leila and myself.

After her recovery, Sandrine was scheduled to return to her seat in the National Assembly on the 16th January 2024. She invited me along with Arielle, Leila and Jeanne to help her prepare a speech for the occasion. Given we had spent months trying to interest elected representatives and political journalists in our cause, we saw this as a crucial opportunity. After all, the National Assembly wrote the laws of the land, and a legislative victory would be a game-changer for us.

This is what she said:

'I have learned that I was drugged without my knowledge. There's a name for this – it's called chemical submission. It's a curse upon society, one that has racked up thousands of victims. From cradle to grave, from office to home, from nightclubs to dinner at a friend's, you're never out of its reach, as its ingredients can be found in every medicine cabinet. Nine out of ten victims are women and 70 per cent of the time they suffer a sexual assault. I stand before you today not simply as a woman chosen as a target, but as a representative chosen by the nation to defend its interests. As such, I am outraged that this subject has been neglected for so long. I ask the government, and specifically the Minister present in this assembly today, to recall a slogan from the 1970s, which has lost none of its pertinence: "Justice must reign for France to be a great nation." Last November, Caroline Darian and the organisation Don't Put Me Under appealed to the government and all other public bodies to work together against chemical submission given the threat it poses to public order, the health of the nation, the exercise of justice, and our educational system. I ask the Minister here today: what is your answer to this heartfelt cry? Will you mobilise the nation's administrative power to help crush this dreadful phenomenon? Will you come to the aid of those intent on exposing its ravages and assuring all of its victims that they will no longer be forgotten? I expect nothing less from you.'

A Breakthrough

Sandrine Josso's demands on our behalf were heard loud and clear. Along with senator Sandrine Guillotin, she was asked by Prime Minister Gabriel Attal to head up a governmental task force on the subject. It brought together experts from many domains, heard hundreds of witnesses speak of their experiences, began to prepare policy recommendations and created an official forum to encourage victims to contribute their stories with a guarantee they would be heard and understood. Don't Put Me Under worked alongside Sandrine throughout this initiative. Unfortunately, two months before the Mazan trial began, a general election was called and the government fell, bringing the task force's endeavours to a premature end.

As soon as news broke of the assault upon Sandrine Josso, she was contacted by hundreds of female victims of chemical submission, intent on sharing their experiences – the isolation and incomprehension, the procedural hurdles in their path, the frustration that their voices were deemed inaudible and the willed deafness of their audience. In Sandrine, who had felt the claws of chemical submission dig into her flesh, these women had finally found someone to whom they could entrust their personal stories.

Despite benefitting from the best possible care and support, Sandrine knew how hard it was to overcome such trauma – to find the courage to rebuild a social life, to face the crush of the Metro, to walk down a street without panicking at the slightest noise, to keep anxiety at bay in the company of unfamiliar men, to reclaim her appetite, to accept dishes prepared by others without fear of what they might conceal, to be patient with her own body and its slow path to recovery.

Every victim of chemical submission should be informed of the host of challenges that await them so that they don't face them alone and unprepared. The path to healing is long and each step requires specific assistance. Even Sandrine, comparatively more fortunate than others, found it hard to receive the right help at the right time. The psychiatrist to whom she was first referred worked out of the same police station in which she had denounced the crime, making each appointment a painful encounter with the past. Quick to realise how triggering this was, she sought out a different specialist for herself.

Sandrine's power lay in her focus on one simple question. First, imagine a victim who is alone, whom nobody believes, who doesn't have access to a hospital able or willing to perform the analysis that would provide concrete proof, who is without an experienced lawyer familiar with the ins and outs of the legal system, who is unprepared for the glacial pace at which the justice system operates, and who is unprepared for the considerable costs involved in building up a credible case. Then ask: how does such a person find justice and repair their life?

The victim accounts flooding into the forum created by the government taskforce convinced both Sandrine and me that their voices were an immensely valuable resource. For a victim, speaking out is a means of survival. Being heard is a first step towards rebuilding. All those they encounter should be taught how to listen and properly process what they hear, whether they are magistrates, lawyers, doctors, pharmacists, nurses, police officers or firemen. When a victim has the courage to speak, society must have the will to act.

The first thing the taskforce did was to issue an open invitation for victims to come forward. On the 21st May 2024 Sandrine Josso opened the first public hearing within the walls of the National Assembly with the words: 'I know only too well that what you have gone through is seared forever in your memories.' The testimony that followed made clear the limits and the failings of the judicial system.

The taskforce demonstrated that geography is a key factor in the quality of response to the crime of chemical submission. Evidence of chemical abuse is far more likely to be collected for those who live in a dense network of highly equipped professionals and institutions such as hospitals, clinics, women's centres and pharmacies. Victims who live far from urban centres usually not only have no concrete proof to support their accusations but also lack access to support networks that prevent the isolation and self-doubt, which can drain victims of the energy and will to seek justice. Sandrine is convinced that, just as hospitals have A&E departments trained and equipped to mobilise all the resources required for a patient in crisis, so too police stations should have a unit primed and ready to receive a victim of chemical submission and immediately capture their testimony. The taskforce's report, even in its incomplete form, contains a raft of such recommendations covering the medical, social, educational and judicial aspects of the problem.

The Centre of Expertise in Substance-Facilitated Abuse was created in 2024 with a nationwide mandate to guide those who suspect themselves to be victims of chemical submission through the institutional maze. It is also responsible for defining and promoting best practice amongst professionals dealing with these situations. Led by Leila Chaouachi, this body represents a huge step forward in the fight against chemical submission.

Although the taskforce was stopped in its tracks by the dissolution of the National Assembly, in October 2024, the Secretary of State for Equality announced that the Prime Minister had mandated Sandrine to continue her investigations into chemical submission, which is now seen as a key priority in the government's programme targeting violence against women.

The Mazan trial had played a large part in the government's waking up to the scale of the problem. It opened the eyes of politicians and the general public, laying bare the sinister mechanisms of the crime. It was a big step forward, but our work with Don't Put Me Under had shown us that good intentions only go so far, and that concrete action is what is really required: changes to the law, and the commitment of significant resources. Bigger victories remain to be won.

* * *

Sandrine Josso is by my side on the train back to Paris after my final appearance at the trial in November 2024. She had come to Avignon as a show of solidarity with me, just as I had waited for her outside the investigating magistrate's office when she was called in to confront Joël Guerriau. While the means at our disposal may be limited, our energy and determination are not. On the train, we discuss drafting a bill for submission to the National Assembly to tackle the scourge of chemical submission and bridge the yawning gap between the existing legal system and the victims.

The following month, a new government is formed, with François Bayrou as Prime Minister. Arielle, Leila, Sandrine and I lobby ceaselessly throughout the course of the trial to ensure that the new administration doesn't satisfy itself with hollow declarations. We want to see a battle plan, built to succeed.

We meet with the leadership team of the National Insurance Board, who decide which medical expenses are reimbursed by the state, to discuss creating a widely available, free-to-use diagnostic kit to facilitate the detection of substances used for chemical submission – a project requiring not just financial backing but the cooperation of countless people and institutions. The National

Agency for the Security of Pharmaceutical Products and the French Hospital Federation asks us to help create a training programme for hospital staff. Discussions are undertaken with the professional bodies representing the labs that do blood work across the country and with the manufacturers of the pharmaceutical substances misused by the predators. Much remains to be done, given our level of ambition, but I begin to believe that 2025 will see tangible, irreversible progress.

When we kicked off our new campaign against chemical submission on 25th November 2024, I wrote the following: 'My goal is that one day soon, anyone who suspects they are a victim can walk into a general practitioner, a pharmacy or a hospital and walk out with a free testing kit after a friction-free and reassuring encounter. By making this essential first step as simple and painless as possible we can help victims overcome their anguish, find the strength to confront their aggressors, and take the first step towards healing their traumatic ordeal.'

We continue to fight tooth and nail for the testing kit. Sandrine was the first to come up with the idea: the equivalent of a compact first aid kit containing the tools required to preserve elements of forensic proof plus a clear guide to the legal process and existing support networks. Such a kit would ensure that evidence was gathered as soon as possible, without waiting for a visit to a police station to register a complaint. Simply by existing, by being widely available, by carrying the official stamp of the nation's health and welfare system, it would demonstrate to victims that they are not alone, their experience neither bizarre nor inexplicable. Crucially, by being fully reimbursed, the kit would dismantle the significant barrier they face today, which requires most victims to pay for tests such as hair sample analysis, which can cost over 1,000 euros.

On 25th November, the Prime Minister announces that kits will soon be freely available through a number of pilot schemes in various areas of the country. The same day, the Health Secretary announces that criminal complaints can henceforth be registered in any hospital with an A&E or gynaecological department.

Progress was being made, but we knew that nothing could have a greater impact than legislative action, so we worked ceaselessly with Sandrine Josso towards this end. Sandrine reached out to a lawyer and former deputy named Emilie Chandler who had previously led a governmental task force on the subject of domestic and inter-familial violence. She too had highlighted the countless judicial obstacles faced by victims and condemned the lack of concern shown by politicians of all parties. She had made many proposals of interest to us: making it possible for judges to issue victims with protection orders within 24 hours of a complaint, creating dedicated teams within judicial tribunals, providing training programmes, and tracking all instances of assaults in a national database. Working with Emilie, we drafted a bill that would support the victims of both chemical submission and domestic and inter-familial violence.

* * *

Andrea Rawlins, a politically engaged film producer, contacted me two years ago, after the French edition of my book opened her eyes to the widespread nature of chemical submission within French society. Convinced that its victims had to be seen and heard, we joined forces to work on a documentary that would tackle the subject head-on. We were determined to show the vast range of victims, from children drugged by their fathers to paralysed but conscious young men imprisoned in their own bodies as they underwent sexual assault. Linda Bendalli, a film director with a well-known production company, immediately signed on to the project.

To convince victims to speak openly on camera, we had to win their trust. We also had to help them acquire the confidence necessary to confront the dizzying feeling of mental blanks when trying to recall what may have happened around losing control of their faculties or the terror of recollections of rape while incapacitated. Every case we unearthed left me shaken and contained elements I recognised from my own experience.

I will cite only two names from amongst so many. Zoé was subjected to chemical submission and rape when 17 years old; now a doctor, she wants chemical submission to feature in the basic training of all student doctors, particularly as students are themselves prime targets for sexual violence. Liwenn, drugged and raped by her father year after year, found the courage to tell a story so harrowing that it haunted me.

We wanted the documentary to be a touchstone for the future, a means through which we could radically change society's perception of sexual aggression and rape. Given the deeply touching feedback from all who have seen the film, it seems that we achieved our goal. It will no longer be possible to dismiss the rape and violence we documented as isolated crimes. We must see the victims as our sisters, our brothers, our mothers, and our friends. That is how I see them, and the terrible trials they have undergone now reside deep within me.

The public broadcasting authority, France Télévisions, agreed to our request to broadcast the documentary during prime time and follow it with a live discussion to drive home the reality of what had been shown. The documentary also found an audience within the educational system, where it serves to warn, protect and arm students against chemical submission. Companies and public bodies have asked permission to screen it internally. It is a powerful means of prevention. By opening eyes and hearts it creates an environment where chemical submission is far less likely to flourish.

I was enormously flattered to receive the backing of The Foundation for Women, created in 2016 by Anne-Cécile Mailfert, one of the most influential and militant feminists in France, and now one of my dearest friends and allies. When The Foundation launched a campaign in 2024 to highlight and denounce sexual violence, she asked me to be one of its heads. Honoured and delighted, I accepted immediately.

As the fight goes on and others join forces with us, the banner raised by Don't Put Me Under has become a rallying point for all. For four long years we fought in the dark, doing everything in our power to expose our sworn enemy from its place, hiding in plain sight. Now that society has come to understand the ubiquity and threat chemical submission represents, we must double down, raising money as we raise awareness, helping today's victims and doing everything to reduce the number of tomorrow's.

We must forge alliances and look further afield. Currently, no other country boasts an organisation like ours, but the need is universal. In Germany, a grassroots investigative organisation called Strg_F successfully unmasked a Telegram chat group dedicated to sharing tips on how best to drug and rape women. More than 70,000 members of the group regularly shared videos of the rapes they had perpetrated and publicised links to sites where the substances used to sedate and immobilise could be purchased.

A worldwide war against chemical submission awaits us, and we are ready to fight it, thanks to all those who have chosen to stand up, say no, and lend us their support.

The Reckoning

On the 19th December 2024, my brothers, my sisters-in-law, my nephew, my husband and I follow my mother and her lawyers out of the courthouse. A police escort holds a swarm of journalists at bay. Thousands of women, and a scattering of men, have been waiting in the street since dawn. We heard them from inside, their defiant slogans and their grateful cries, heartfelt thanks for standing up for them, defending their rights, giving them strength.

I walk through the crowd along with some members of my family and my editor.

I drink in the sight and sound of all these women, who have shown solidarity and been present since the start of the trial, and think of the comments aimed at them by the defence lawyers: 'hysterical women', 'foul-mouthed shrews' and 'bloodthirsty vultures'. Many victims were drawn here by their violent personal history. Many have been fighting this battle for a long time. They all see themselves in our mother, for whom they have come bearing their love and compassion. I am at one with them, but although I wish I could thank them, share in their smiles and believe in their chants of victory, I am too numb to do so.

It took three and a half hours for the verdicts to be handed down and the sentences announced. Justice has spoken, but it did so in terms that came as a blow to us and all the other victims and left a bitter taste in the mouth. The court ignored the demands of the prosecution and handed out watered-down sentences. The accused and their lawyers cannot hide their relief and their self-satisfied smiles. As for my brother David and I, we cannot hide our revulsion.

I walk from the courtroom asking myself: is this what passes for justice? Is justice not just blind but tone deaf?

Dominique is declared guilty on all charges. He is sentenced to 20 years' imprisonment, two thirds of which must be served before any remission or reduction of sentence can be considered.

None of the pleas of innocence from the co-accused have been accepted. They are all found guilty, for the most part of aggravated rape (the aggravating factors being group rape and/or rape with administration of illegal substances).

The court has given short shrift to the argument from the accused and their lawyers that although their deeds were objectively wrong, the perpetrators themselves lacked criminal intention. Only one of those sentenced is recognised as having diminished capacity. Despite this, the co-accused receive much milder sentences than those sought by the prosecution. Six of them are allowed to walk out of the court and go home, rather than to prison.

Some commentators and legal specialists describe the result as a triumph for equitable justice – that the sentences have been tailored to individual circumstances, such as the number of rapes committed, the presence or absence of explicit knowledge of my mother's sedated state, the presence or absence of a previous criminal record, and the social and familial circumstances of the accused. I'm inclined to believe that the court chose to draw a dubious and dangerous distinction between Dominique Pelicot and the others. Since he was the conductor of the sinister symphony, they were simply following the commands of his baton. Since his guilt was absolute, theirs had to be less so.

The co-accused received sentences that, on the whole, were shorter than those handed out in most rape trials in France. After all that had been revealed during the four months of the trial, it is no wonder that the outcome leaves so many shell-shocked.

My brothers and I are disappointed by the result, to put it mildly. As this was supposed to have been a historic trial, does that mean the outcome shows the direction in which history is heading?

It has been said that the court rendered justice.

I believe that justice was not delivered. I believe that our voices weren't properly heard. I believe that the court failed to understand that the perpetrator of the crime was not just a man but was chemical submission itself – tellingly, the expression 'chemical submission' figured in none of the sentences handed down. I believe the court failed to grasp the menace chemical submission represents to women and society as a whole. I believe that the defence lawyers had good reason to smile to themselves at the end. We had been warned that the all the accused might react with anger to their sentences. All I saw was cynical delight.

Six men walked out of the courtroom, guilty but free to go home. Some of them ploughed triumphantly through the crowd outside, insulting the women who had stood by Gisèle. What did they take away from the trial? Will they now simply remove it from their minds? Have they learned anything? Have they grasped the reality of what they did?

Do they understand that they are, and always will be, rapists and that they do not deserve our forgiveness?

So many seem to believe that Dominique's sentence was exemplary. They should, like me, listen to Florence Rault, whose prediction is chilling: if he benefits from the standard probation process and he is not brought to trial for the assaults on Sophie Narme and Marion, then he could leave prison far sooner than anyone expects. Despite his appalling crimes, he will not die behind bars. Who could be happy with that?

Setting aside the verdicts and the sentences, it was the spectacle that played out at the close of the trial that left my brothers and I dumbstruck. We watched the defence lawyers congratulating each other and exchanging high-fives. We recoiled inwardly as some of them flippantly wished us a Merry Christmas and Happy New Year. Faced with their indecent glee, my thoughts turned, as ever, to the victims, to all those who have brought their experiences of rape to a courtroom and had to endure something akin to this.

Although this was supposed to be an exceptional event in the annals of judicial history, the Mazan proceedings turned out to be just another rape trial.

My mother, whose status as victim was indubitable – her tormenter having confessed, and her suffering having been documented by hundreds of photos and videos – was nonetheless treated with suspicion and contempt in court by the defence lawyers. Shocking to witness, but standard practice in a rape trial. Like all other victims of rape and sexual aggression, to the defence this suggested that she must have been a little guilty, a little complicit, because aren't they all?

As in any other trial, my brothers and I were fair game, shamelessly slapped about verbally by the defence. Wasn't our supposed torment clearly a bit exaggerated? Wasn't I – just like the actress Adèle Haenel, whose denunciations of sexual abuse in the film industry were in the headlines at the time – over-indulging in anger? Didn't I understand the etiquette of a courtroom? Couldn't I hold my tongue and still my pen? Did I really have to be so undignified? Like all other victims of rape and sexual aggression, I had to be exaggerating, I would have done better to stay silent, I should have known my place and not made waves.

As in any other trial, my brothers and I felt that our own lawyers had let us down. In their fight for Gisèle they had been impeccable, but, as my brother observed the day after the verdict, we – David, Céline, Florian, Aurore, Nathan and myself – were all civil parties to the prosecution, and, as such, should have been counselled, consulted and kept fully informed from start to finish. It wasn't just Gisèle's trial, it was that of an entire family devastated by Dominique Pelicot. When my brothers, my sister-in-law and I stopped attending the trial after the first few weeks, returning to our jobs and families, we were cut out by the lawyers. They stopped sending accounts of the proceedings, debriefs, comments and explanations. Left to our own devices, there was no one to explain what was really happening, what was important and what was not, and what we should expect. When the sentences were announced, we had no context in which to interpret them.

At a critical moment after the verdict, we found ourselves lost and abandoned. Not understanding what would happen next, we staggered into the hall outside the courtroom, missing the moment when Dominique was solemnly removed and taken back to prison. When we returned to the courtroom, the dock was empty. A moment of great symbolic importance had been stolen from us.

After the verdict, Gisèle and her two lawyers left the courthouse under police escort, moved slowly through the crowd and climbed into a waiting car which whisked them away. Having followed behind them, my brothers and I were left at the kerb. We walked on alone, our shoulders slumped, lost in silence. An end had come to four years of waiting and four months of courtroom drama. Where could we turn now?

We had hoped so much that the Mazan trial would break the mould. It didn't.

There was a telling moment on that final day when the presiding judge seemed lost. He spoke hesitantly and in a feeble voice, walking back his words upon realising that he had made a mistake, presenting his excuses to one of the accused whose name he had called in error. That's how I now think of the justice system: prone to error and full of excuses.

If radical change – for that alone will answer our hopes and our demands – is to come, then it will have to come from elsewhere.

But from where, when and for whom?

What has the trial achieved? What lessons has it taught us – particularly when we already know that 17 of those found guilty have already appealed their convictions, and that a new trial is scheduled for the 29th September 2025?

David said it first: 'This trial should be a reference point for future generations and a beacon showing the way, particularly for our sons.'

The trial is ours. Yours, mine, ours.

It concerns us as parents, as women and men, as victims, as distant observers and first-hand witnesses. It contains lessons for us all, dilemmas we must resolve, and resolutions we must follow through. It points to what justice should be, how sex education should be conducted at home and in school, how violence should be prevented, and to how we should fight against chemical submission, rape culture, incest and the corrosive effects of online pornography. We are all concerned because the Mazan trial has demonstrated that nowhere is safe. Criminals undertake violent abuse, generally with impunity, within our families, within our couples, within our workplaces, within bars and clubs, on the streets, on social networks, and in every corner of the web.

During these long and difficult weeks, I talked endlessly with Florence Rault about the law and the legal system, about the proper role of defence lawyers, about the contribution of civil parties to the prosecution, about the place reserved for victims. The behaviour and stance of some of the defence lawyers in the Avignon courthouse had been egregious, given their aggressive questions and shameless insinuations that Gisèle could have been Dominique Pelicot's accomplice. They were the ones who insisted that some of the acts committed should be regarded as rapes in name only, that my mother – violated by two men while unconscious – could be talked of as having participated in a 'three-way sex game', that Gisèle appeared to consent because 'her legs were bent and her lower body seemed to move to provide a more comfortable position'. At what point does a lawyer cease to be the level-headed defender of his client's rights and become yet another persecutor of his client's victim?

The European Court of Human Rights has a clear position on this point: a victim should not be victimised in the courtroom. Its ruling appears to have had little effect on actual practice. How many victims have felt, like Gisèle, that they have undergone a second assault while being cross-examined by defence lawyers? How many lawyers defend their client without attempting to convince the court that their victim was either responsible for, or complicit in, their own rape? Who endeavours to treat victims with justice and humanity at every step in their quest for justice, from filing a complaint and confronting their aggressor before an investigating magistrate, to the endless and exhausting days of the trial, if and when it finally comes around?

Sometimes a simple error of judgement can harm a victim, such as when Béatrice Zavarro wound up her defence of Dominique by quoting the so-called poems he wrote in prison, offered as an indication of his remorse for the depths to which he had fallen. Or when, on his behalf, she asked us, his children, to remember only his good side and filter out the rest. Some things should never be said because they are not fit to be heard.

The Mazan trial invites us to rethink some fundamental questions. What is just in absolute terms, and how can justice be meted out in a practical way? How can victims be best protected from the hard knocks that they will inevitably encounter in their pursuit of justice? What can be done for the victims deprived of proof of the crimes they have suffered?

One of the defence lawyers deliberately sought to provoke the crowd outside the courtroom after the verdict: 'My client is walking away a free man! A free man! ... He has a message for all you hysterical and foul-mouthed women. Here it is: Up yours! With a smile, of course, you vengeful ghouls!' He failed to anticipate the quick wit of the women before him. Borrowing from the lawyer who had insisted 'there's rape, and then there's rape', they replied: 'There are lawyers, and then there are lawyers.' They couldn't have been more right.

* * *

I'm not a lawyer. I'm not an elected representative sitting in the National Assembly. I don't know whether changing the law on rape to add an explicit reference to the presence or absence of consent would be judicious or, as some insist, dangerous. But I do know that what we need as a matter of urgency is a law that defends and protects victims, and ensures they are not forgotten. Sandrine Josso and the Foundation for Women are working on a draft bill designed to better protect victims. It remains to be seen whether the government and the National Assembly will finally admit the importance of what's at stake and clear a path for such an initiative.

I will never forget that the trial would not have happened if a decent man, driven by a sense of duty and outrage at what he'd seen, had not arrested Dominique in a supermarket and asked the three women he had been stalking to file complaints against him. This anonymous man – a humble security guard in a Carpentras supermarket who refused to look the other way because, in his own words, he 'didn't want the creep to get away with it' – deserves all our thanks. He certainly has mine.

I'll never forget that not a single man lured by Dominique to his house in Mazan, or to mine, thought to denounce what he discovered. Although some claim to have been troubled by the experience – regretting after the fact, in their weasel words, their 'poor judgement' – they all went quietly back home and got on with their lives, fully aware that a woman was imprisoned in an endless cycle of abuse a few kilometres from them and their families.

I'll never forget courage of the few and the gutlessness of the many. Or the misogyny of an entire society.

I'll never forget the failings and the incompetence that left Dominique untroubled for years while the police did nothing with the DNA sample they'd taken from him. I'll never forget the relentless and disciplined work of the investigators who revealed the vast extent of Dominique's crimes after his arrest in 2020 and ensured that he and others answered for at least part of what they had done.

I'll never forget my mother's anguish and her strength. In bearing her cross, she took upon her shoulders the suffering of legions of women. Through her, they finally became visible and found their voices.

I'll never forget that I remain alone with the consequences of the crime I suffered, my distress discounted, my cries unheard. I'll never forget the trauma inflicted by incest on so many families, and the sinister way it is reborn from generation to generation.

I'll never forget Dominique's other victims, including all those who remain invisible through lack of evidence.

I'll never forget the battles we've fought and those we've yet to win.

I want to – and will – remember everything.

If the trial is to be, as my brother David said, a beacon showing the way forward for our children, my thoughts turn to my son, to all he has inherited and the future that awaits him.

We must speak up, we must show our anger, we must step forward, we must defend our rights and extend the fight to new fronts. We must talk to our families and our friends, breaking the law of silence, overthrowing taboos, and replacing solitude with solidarity. We must fight, fight and fight again. We must overcome fear and uncertainty to focus on the future. I have no idea how we will evolve and how we learn to live with our scars. We each have to come to terms with the loss of our former selves and seek a new way of being. We have no other option because we have to believe that things have indeed changed. The eyes of the world have been opened to crimes that had gone unnoticed, to rape and abuse that had not been punished, to forgotten women who had been left to fight unseen and unaided.

Let them feel they are no longer alone. Let them be heard and believed. Let them know they have our unending support.

Acknowledgements

I wish to thank, from the depths of my heart:

My brothers, David and Florian, and my sister-in-law, Céline, a true sister to me, for never once letting me out of their sight.

My closest friends Inga, Carole, Marion and Aurélie for standing by me without fail since this ordeal began.

My husband and my son, whom I love more than anyone or anything in this world.

My French publishers JC Lattès, particularly Véronique Cardi and the ever-attentive Anne-Sophie Stefanini for having helped and guided me through every step of the writing of this book.